WONDER TALES OF
ANCIENT WALES

WONDER TALES OF ANCIENT WALES

BY

BERNARD HENDERSON
AND STEPHEN JONES

ILLUSTRATED BY
DORIS WILLIAMSON AND CONSTANCE E. ROWLANDS

JOHN JONES

WONDER TALES OF ANCIENT WALES

Re-published at Ruthin, North Wales, October 1998

First published 1921 by Philip Allan & Co, London

Written by Bernard Henderson and Stephrn Jones

Illustrations by Doris Williamson and Constance E. Rowlands

ISBN 1 871083 90 7

Cover design by Olwen Fowler, Roch, Pembrokeshire

Printed by C.I.T. Printing Services Ltd, Merlins Bridge, Haverfordwest, Pembrokeshire SA61 1XF

Published by JOHN JONES PUBLISHING LTD, Unit 12, Clwydfro Business Centre, Ruthin, North Wales, LL15 1NJ

PREFACE

THE Stories in this book are told entirely in our own words and according to our own methods, and we believe that a large proportion of them have not appeared hitherto in an English garb. One of them, namely, ' Llew,' has never been seen before in any attire, for it is new-born.

We went to Welsh literature, and, having borrowed the underlying ideas of certain attractive stories, we placed them, so far as language is concerned, in an English setting, which, allowing for difference of idiom and word, represents sufficiently the sentiment and colour of the Welsh original. It follows, therefore, that the reader may at times possess what is practically a direct translation, or again, it may be that he is perusing what our imagination has supplied to heighten effect or fill out a slender outline.

Our earnest hope is that the result of our joint labour—this Welsh spirit speaking through an English voice—will win the benison both of the critic and of the general public.

The pronunciation and meaning of the proper names are indicated phonetically in footnotes, and the syllable to be stressed is usually marked by an acute (′) accent. ' ū ' is always pronounced like the ' oo ' in ' pool,' and ' dd ' like the ' th ' in ' this.' ' Oi ' is a diphthong, and the short (˘) and long (–) marks indicate the volume of the vowels.

CONTENTS

PLATES IN COLOUR

DRAWINGS IN TEXT

WONDER TALES OF ANCIENT WALES

I

LLEW [1]

LONG, long ago, in the village of Pennant, there lived two very poor people who had one little boy named Llew. They were so poor that Llew had to feed on the coarsest food, and he wore scarcely any clothes at all. But that did not trouble him. He was as happy as the day is long, and in the warm summer time he tumbled about amongst the rich hay, while in winter he rolled in the snow, or perhaps climbed the tall trees to keep himself warm.

One golden summer morning, as he was pushing along through a big swathe of hay, he came to a place where a circle of rich grass grew, under the stems that had fallen before the mowers' scythes. His eyes lit upon a tiny old man, whose clothing

[1] Lleu, lion.

had got entangled in some thorns. He was the quaintest little thing Llew had ever seen. His coat was blue; and he wore a curious cap fashioned out of skins, while his legs were enclosed in trousers which also covered his feet and came out to a point at his toes. Sad, blinding tears were trickling down his face, his mouth was

" A TINY OLD MAN . . . ENTANGLED IN SOME THORNS."

puckered into sorrowful lines, and his snowy beard lay in confusion over his shoulders. Yet his face was kind, and the boy felt not the slightest fear.

" Hullo ! " said Llew. " Who are you ? "

" Oh ! please set me free," cried the little old man.

" Of course I will ! " replied Llew, who was a kind little fellow. " But what's your name ? "

As he said this he gently picked the thorns away from the little man's coat till he was quite at liberty.

" Thank you, Llew," he said ; and sat down on a wisp of hay. " Now you want to know my name, and who I am ? Well, I'm one of a large family called the Tylwyth Têg.[1] We live somewhere not far from here, and we love all people who are kind, and hate those who are cruel, and since there is kindness in your heart so that you have done me good service, whenever you may chance to be in trouble, sing to us, and my kith and kin will be sure to try to help you." And, when he had spoken, he sang a sweet, abiding tune which sank into the lad's heart as the song of the thrush gladdens the traveller in the early springtide.

> " Little lad, my little lad,
>   Sing for your friend,
>   When your heart is very sad,
>   My help I'll send.
>   And wheresoever you may be,
>   When you sing your friend you'll see."

And lo ! when the song was sung he vanished, and the boy could no longer see him. Yet it seemed to Llew that music still stole in sweet melody

[1] Téllûith Taig, Family fair.

around the circle of rich grass. He went to his home humming the tune softly to himself.

Very soon afterwards poverty fell even more bitterly upon the poor parents, and they had to send their little boy away to earn his living. They put him with a shoemaker, who lived in a town a long way off, for they thought that if Llew learned how to make boots and shoes he might earn bread for himself in the coming years.

And now the poor boy had a most unhappy time. His master was harsh and cruel as the sharp east wind, and beat his miserable little servant unmercifully ; and, though the boy tried his hardest, he could not do anything to please the man. Indeed, the more he tried to please him the more heavily the cruel blows fell. It takes a very long time to learn to make boots and shoes, and Llew's master, who was far from being a clever man himself, seemed to think that his young servant ought to acquire the skill quite easily. Yes, and dull people are often very unfair, for they lack the knowledge which, like a key, opens the door to another's heart.

One day this dull creature had gone out, leaving Llew a great deal of work to do, and he told him that if it were not all finished by the time he came back he would beat him severely.

" And this time, my boy, you shall be black and blue all over."

Poor little Llew !

The salt tears would come, in spite of his efforts to be brave and do his work, and they fell like the rain which comes from the dark, heavy clouds of the west. Then his sad thoughts travelled to the warm summer fields. He seemed to see the gentle sunshine kissing the delicate leaves as they tossed merrily on the passing breeze ; he heard the silvery stream bickering over the rounded stones, and, almost without knowing what words his lips were framing, he sang from his heart these words of the Tylwyth Têg :

> " Tiny folk as fair as down !
>   Llew's heart is sad.
> Quit the country, seek the town,
>   And make me glad.
> Come and sing a merry lay,
> Where you dance there's no dismay."

Then lo ! before the last words had left his trembling lips, truly a strange sight passed before his wondering eyes, and he seemed to be in a strange place rather than in the dirt-stained work-room of the harsh shoemaker. The room was full of the Tylwyth Têg, dancing and jigging over the leather shavings. Gleefully they climbed up the bench and twinkled in merry sport in and out among the old tools. In appearance they were all so much alike that he could not be certain which was his special friend, until *he* came up, and, in a soft and comforting voice said, " Why didn't you sing before ? We cannot come unless you sing."

Then, before Llew could reply, the tiny man had skipped away and was hard at work with his comrades. Their little hands sped like the shuttle in the loom, and their voices rose merrily as the song of a bird in a grove when the daylight has driven dark night over the edge of the world. How they worked ! and how they sang ! Before a hungry horse could eat a nosebagful of oats all the work was done, and in such a way as no shoe-maker on earth could do it.

" Now," said the chief of the Tylwyth Têg, a merry, blue-eyed old fellow with a smile like the mellow autumn, " that's all right for the present ; but, my lad, you must be taught to work like this yourself. We will show you ! " Thereupon they seized his fingers, and beneath their gentle guidance he soon found himself working almost as skilfully as they did. " Good ! Very good ! " they cried, and wagged their heads in knowing manner.

Then from the village street there came the noise of a rambling footstep, and a heavy tread was heard coming along the stone passage. The tiny folk vanished as wonderfully as they had come. Llew's master flung open the door and burst into the room.

" Now then ! " he said in drunken hoarseness, picking up a strap as he spoke, " I'll show you ! "

Even as he spoke his glance fell upon four beautiful pairs of shoes lying finished on the bench.

" What ! " he gasped. " You didn't—— But you must have ! Good gracious ! " and he dropped the strap from his coarse, dirty fingers.

After this Llew's master grew to be the richest man in the town ; but he never thanked Llew. His gratitude lay locked in his heart as the water is gripped by winter's frost. Rather he was harder than ever, and the little fellow's heart was often downcast. But the people of the town said that the shoemaker had never made such boots before Llew came ; and they loved the boy, and were very kind to him.

Now it chanced one day that the king of that realm went hunting the wild creatures that lived in the woods near the town where Llew dwelt, and, while he was riding in much haste, he fell and tore his riding-boots, so that he came into town and asked for a shoemaker. The townsfolk led him to Llew's master, for they explained to the king that he would find at that shop such boots as even a king might wear. As the king entered the shop the man bowed low, and when he had received the royal order he smiled in cunning wise, and then went out. Coming to the low shed where the poor boy sat bravely at his work, he struck him violently and shouted :

" Now then, set to work and let me have the best boots you can make."

Then he stood and waited till Llew had finished, and in eager haste carried them back himself.

Placing before the king the boots, which were perfect in size and workmanship, he said humbly :

" There they are, your Majesty," and knelt in lowly reverence upon the floor.

" HE PUT HIS HAND DOWN TO HIS LEG."

When he saw the boots, the king was lost in astonishment, and exclaimed :

" Well, you are the cleverest workman I have ever seen ! But stay ! Did you make them yourself ? "

Then the shoemaker made answer, " Yes, sire ; I—— " but lo ! there burst from his lips an awful scream, and in great haste he put his hand down to his leg. For, all unseen, one of the Tylwyth Têg, hearing the false words, had run a long, sharp needle right through his stocking into his stubborn flesh. But the shoemaker, feeling the bewildered glance of the king was upon him, made haste to recover himself, and said, " I crave your Majesty's pardon. Yes, indeed, sire, I made—— " There came an agonizing scream, vastly louder than before, and he yelled and danced in prolonged agony.

" Come now ! " said the king, growing suspicious, " did you really make them your-self ? "

Then the shoemaker, in dread of another agony, did not again attempt to deceive, but went in shame and anger, and bringing Llew presented him to the king, who was astonished to find so young a boy so clever a craftsman. He left orders that Llew was to go and dwell at the palace, and be shoemaker to the royal family.

Then the lad remembered the old folks at home and sent them gifts from his abundance. Often as he lay in his soft, warm bed, there would come in the stillness of the night a tiny voice which sang in his ear :

> " Little Llew, you shall be King !
> Some day, some day,

You must make a fairy ring
  Where we can play,
In the night when watch dogs sleep,
And the stars all silent creep.

Near your palace build a wall
  Round gardens bright ;
Plant the foxgloves gay and tall,
  The hemlock white,
Willow herb and crane-bill's lance—
Where the Tylwyth Têg may dance."

And, when several years had rolled away over the distant mountains, and dropped silently into the mist beyond the ocean, the words of the song were fulfilled.

In time the king of the realm went to war. " Make yourself a pair of shoes as fast as the wind," was whispered to Llew, " and stand forth as the king's messenger." The tiny folk gave him a wonderful coat wrought skilfully of gossamer thread so that none might see him when he wore it. Hither and thither sped Llew through the ways of war, gathering news for the king. Unseen he passed through the enemy's camp, learned their plans as they framed them in secrecy, and bore the tidings to his royal master. When red blood had ceased to flow, and the dogs of war fled speedily from the land, the king rode in triumph to his palace, and made Llew his chief minister ; but, honoured with titles, and dignified with rank, the youth still won everybody's love

by his kindness and thoughtfulness. Among
others who loved him was the king's fair daughter,
and after a time they were joined in wedlock. So,
when the old king passed away to his forefathers
and lay silent in death's long sleep, Llew reigned
in his stead.

But he always remembered the gentle kindness

" . . . LITTLE FOLK, DANCING HAND IN HAND."

of the Tylwyth Têg. Outside his palace there was
a beautiful garden, stocked with fragrant roses
and all the fair flowers that grow in the meadows,
or by the river-side. Silvery fountains leapt
gleaming and sparkling in the rays of the sun, and
little murmuring streams flowed merrily along.
People said that sometimes when the moon was

silver bright, if anyone peeped over the wall of that garden there might be seen a band of many little folk, dancing hand in hand through the drops that fell glittering in the moonlight.

When Llew heard this he smiled. Perhaps it was true. What do you think about it ?

II

BWCA'R TRWYN [1]
OR
THE BIG-NOSED BOGIE

WHERE he came from nobody knew, but there he was without any doubt. When the farm servants met together round the nut-brown ale of a Saturday night, each one had strange tales to tell of what had happened during the week. One man told how somebody had pinched him on the back of the neck, and on turning round to see who it was, lo! there was empty air and a mocking laugh. A maid had heard a terrible noise in the cowhouse, and, rushing to see what it was, she just caught sight of a brown, hairy hand disappearing through a chink in the opposite wall; and so the tales went on. But one girl never said a word. She simply sat mum. The other folk glanced at her from time to time in a meaning sort of way; but she took no notice. She was, indeed, a very strange sort of girl. Her name was Mari, and they called her Modryb Mari.[2]

[1] Būka-r-truin, bogey of the nose.
[2] Modrib Mary, Aunt Mary.

No one knew anything at all about Mari save that the mistress had bought her at the fair, and people said that she was one of the Bendith y Mamau.[1] Before she had come to the farm everything had gone on in quite an ordinary way ; but from the moment of her arrival these strange things began to happen. A cow had spoken like a man. The Sunday cake had a big stone in the middle of it, and the stockings of the farmer's wife were always found in the morning tied in a knot. People said that when the house was quiet at night time a sturdy goblin used to come, and, stretched out full length, bask himself to sleep before the fire. In the morning, after drinking up the remainder of the milk, he popped out of doors before anyone could catch him. And, somehow or other, all these things were put down to Modryb Mari.

Well, the truth of the whole matter was that Mari and the goblin were capital friends, and quite understood each other. No maid on the farm worked less than Mari, and yet no one did more than she. This was because she understood the goblin so well.   For he was the cleverest goblin the world has ever known, although no one realized at the time that he had such a huge nose. That was discovered much later on ; but we shall find out about his nose in due course. Mari understood all about his cleverness long before she came to the farm. They were old friends ; and but for

[1] Bendith e mamei, blessing of the mothers.

Mari's foolishness might have remained so to the end of the chapter. That is really the worst thing about women all the world over. They are too inquisitive, and too much inclined to be rather hard on their best friends. At any rate so it was with Mari.

This goblin could turn his hand to anything. He washed the clothes for Mari, and they looked as white as driven snow. He ironed, and the linen was never so much as scorched. He span wool and twisted it into skeins; his work at the spinning-wheel was wonderful. The wheel flew round at a furious rate and the thread never snapped while he was spinning. Bwca did all this work and much more besides—dusting, washing-up, milking— there was no end to all his cleverness ; and he did it all for Mari.

But goblins, like human beings, must be rewarded for their toil. Even an honest man will look out anxiously for pay-day, and Bwca liked a pay-day every day, for he had a weakness, a most decided weakness, for bread and milk. It is true that cream was a great favourite of his, especially the top-skimming ; but bread and milk was the real stuff for him. He liked it warm with some sugar. That was all the wages Bwca desired ; and that was all Mari gave him. Each night as she went up to bed she placed the bowl of bread and milk at the foot of the stairs for him to come and fetch when he was ready. This had gone on

for such a time it was no wonder that the other
servants looked askance, or that strange things
happened when Mari came to the farm.

Now if Mari had been wise she would have
raised Bwca's wages rather than have tried to cheat
the poor goblin out of his bread and milk.   But, as
you have heard, she was too inquisitive ; and this
was the reason.   Never since they had been
partners had she seen this hard-working goblin,
never once.   She left the full bowl by the stairs
at night ; and she picked it up empty in the
morning.   All the work that had to be done
stood waiting in the kitchen, and, sure enough,
next morning the wool was spun and twisted,
or the sewing finished.   Sometimes she said,
" Bwca, what are you like to look at ? "   And
then Bwca used to go away without giving any
reply.

So one sad night, after such a disappearance,
Mari, out of mere spite, put in the bowl some brine
in which a ham had been soaking for a week, and
left the brew for Bwca's supper.   Foolish maid
that she was, for dire and lasting trouble came
speedily upon her.   At the first mouthful by the
kitchen fire Bwca's face had twisted in all directions
at once, and his furry, pointed ears had stuck up as
straight as a dog's tail.   " Faugh ! ugh ! p-p-pla ! "
he said, and dashed the bowl to the ground in fury.
Then he stood behind the kitchen door, and never
budged all night.

In the morning down came Mari. No empty bowl by the stairs ; dust on the floor ; and through the open door of the scullery a vision of last night's supper things still unwashed ! She turned the handle of the kitchen door in haste, when oh ! what a terrible trouble came upon her ! The

" MARI RAN . . . SHRIEKING FOR HELP."

goblin was waiting there patiently. He sprang out, seized her by the scruff of her neck, and screamed in anger :

" To think of your giving me brine instead of my bread and milk ! After all that I have done for you ! You hoiden ! You wretched gipsy ! I'll twist your neck for you ! No more sticks I'll

3

fetch for firing ! Brine ! The idea of it ! " So he went on, and as he spoke he kicked, and as he kicked he pinched and scratched.

With her hands over her ears to shut out the din and ward off the blows Mari ran from the room shrieking for help. And after her went Bwca, kicking, raving, and red with anger.

" Help ! help ! " cried the wretched girl.

" I'll make you call for help," screamed Bwca, and flung himself upon her shoulders and hammered away with his fists.

After some time Mari's cries woke up the other servants ; they came rushing downstairs, pell mell, to find Mari sitting on the floor, her face black and blue and scratched miserably, her hair (such as was left) twisted almost out of her head. Bwca had gone, and no one at the farm ever saw him again.

But Bwca had to live—even goblins must eat ; and for two years people in the neighbourhood missed things. Food disappeared at night : now it was cheese ; now a roasted fowl ; another time a dish of custard ; and suspicion always pointed its finger at the poor Elf. Then it would seem that he went to live at Hafod yr Ynys,[1] where he struck up a warm friendship with Eilian Elis. Eilian was crafty, for she knew all about Mari's misfortune. So she fed the little goblin as though he were a turkey cock. Warm bread and milk

[1] Havod er Innis, summer dwelling of the island.

never failed him, and sometimes there was a piece of butter and some treacle. Other tit-bits came as well, so life was paradise for Bwca. He span wool, he wound yarn, and the spinning-wheel worked so swiftly that if it had not been a first-class piece of machinery it would have been torn to pieces. No brine for Bwca at Hafod yr Ynys. Not so ! but the fat of the land, milk and honey, and the first cut from the joint. Yet affliction came to him even there.

It came in this manner :

" What is your name, dear ? " asked Eilian Elis one day.

" Never you mind that," quoth Bwca. " That's my affair."

" But, sweetheart, do tell me," said Eilian.

" I will not," said Bwca.

" Not if I give you a basin of bread and milk twice as large for your supper, Lovey ? "

" Not if you give me everything ! " was the reply.

Then Eilian, with the cunning of her sex, took refuge in artfulness. One evening as the men and maids went out, and Bwca took up his task at the spinning-wheel, she made as though she were going out also, and banging the kitchen door, stood in silence outside. As he began to spin, he sang in a low, deep voice a sort of chant :

> " The maid would laugh could she but win
> To know my name is Bwca'r Trwyn."

Open flew the door, and from the foot of the stairs the stupid Eilian shrilled out :

"OPEN FLEW THE DOOR."

" Well ! Bwca'r Trwyn ! What a name, to be sure ! "

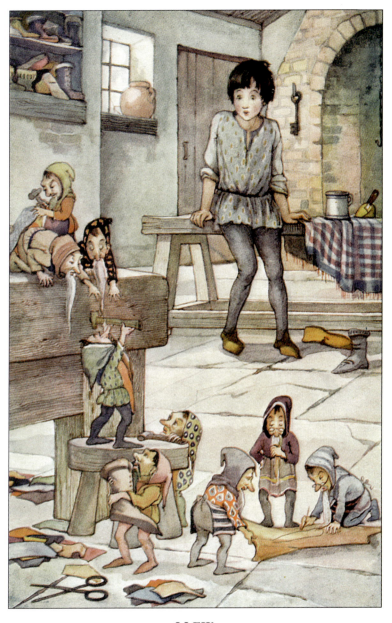

LLEW

"The room was full of the Tylwyth Teg, dancing and jigging all over the leather shavings."

(Plate 1)

BWCA'R TRWYN

"Each night as she went up to bed she placed the bowl of bread and milk at the foot of the stairs for him." *(Plate 2)*

There was a crash, a howl of pain, and Bwca had gone for ever from Hafod yr Ynys. The spinning-wheel was smashed to atoms.

The world was not kind to poor Trwyn, was it? But worse was to follow. For a time he companied with Evan, a serving-man at a farm not very far away, and did him many a good turn till Evan had to go away to fight against Richard Crookback. Sad to tell, he was killed on Bosworth Field, and, as his friend did not return, Bwca began to be a mischance to the farmer. Sometimes when the oxen were ploughing an unseen hand would turn them round in the middle of the field. The cows trod in the milk pail; the bee-hive was overturned; two cows were found with their tails knotted together; the milkmaid dared not go alone to the milking-shed; a calf was born with three eyes. Pranks and mischief never ceased, until the farmer waxed desperate and determined to ask help of the priest from the village in the valley. The priest asked many questions: Had anyone seen the goblin? How long had this mischief continued? Had he ever injured anyone? Did he ever speak? When the priest had learned all he could, he arose with a very grave look on his face. Taking his candle, his bell, and his book he motioned to the farmer to lead the way to the farm.

When they drew near the farm, the moon was shining at the full and the night was very warm, for it was Midsummer Eve. Just as they entered the house a long, low, cunning laugh was heard from the store cupboard. It was the laugh of one who has found what he has long been seeking, and, having found, is full of contentment. So they went on tiptoe and looked in through the keyhole. The goblin was sitting on a shelf, with

" GULPING DOWN GREAT HANDFULS."

a bowl of bread and milk on his knees, gulping down great, dripping, greedy handfuls, while the milk was trickling down his hairy chin.

" Lock the door," whispered the priest, and the farmer obeyed.

" Now we have him," whispered the priest ; " but, before I begin, fetch an awl."

So the farmer fetched one. Then the priest, in deep, commanding accents, began to read, and, as he read, he rang his bell in steady, slow movement. There was a sound of scuffling in the pantry, followed by a hard push at the door. But still the good priest read steadily the glorious words of his holy book, and never ceased ringing his bell, while the farmer held the candle for him to see what was written. A howl came from within, and dishes were dashed on the ground. The farmer could distinctly hear the big milk jug fall crashing to the floor.

" Let me out ! " screamed Bwca'r Trwyn.

But the priest went on reading. The noise was now terrific, and a loud crash on the panel of the door split the wood, and through the gap appeared Bwca's long nose. In a moment the farmer had run an awl through the nose from one side to the other, and the deed was done. Bwca was a captive ; and there he remained, fuming, yet firmly fixed, till the calm and holy man had finished chanting the words that freed the land from the lubber fiend.

" In the name of St. Francis and St. Benedict I command thee to haste to the banks of the Red Sea, O Goblin. Appear not in the sight of man till fourteen generations (yea, mark, twice seven, that holy number) have come and gone. Thou shalt pass hither by the upper wind, so that, as thou wendest thy way, thou shalt cause no harm or hindrance to the sons of men.   Avaunt, and quit my sight ! "

As the priest spoke these words a loud wind began to sweep around the house till the fabric shook to its foundation.   Screaming, wailing noises were heard, and the farmer hid his face in his hands.   But the priest took hold of the awl, drew it from Bwca's nose, and stood aside.   Out fled the goblin with a scream of impotent anger, and so passed into the night.

Such was the power of the priest that never since in that neighbourhood has sprite or goblin troubled house or shelter or food of any kind. Yet sometimes, when the wind is high, there comes down from the hills a low wailing, and then men who are wise close every door and window in the house, and build big fires on the hearth.

III

THE SEA-MAIDEN

EVERY day in the week, on Sundays and Holy-days as well as workadays, Ifan [1] Morgan would be down by the sea feasting his eyes on the dancing, glancing waves. Before the first trembling light began to turn the eastern sky a pearly grey, and before the bush-birds gave their first sleepy tweet-tweet, Ifan was wending his way to the waves. Nor was this strange, for Ifan's forefathers had done the same thing; and, in his childhood, he had seen his father fishing in the sea, or watching from the shore. And so Ifan Morgan was like his fore-fathers. Sometimes in the season he went to catch the frisky mackerel, or the silver herring when it came in shoals near the coast. But his chief delight was to walk along the sea-shore and see what good things his uncle Dafy Jones would bring him; for that was the name by which the Morgans called the great wide sea.

One morning, just as the first pale blue of the dawn stole out of the night, Ifan sat by the great

[1] Ivan, John.

25

yawning mouths of the dark caves that lay under the hill-sides. His eyes seemed busy searching for something that could not be found, and, ever and anon, they wandered towards, and dwelt upon the cave of Deio.[1] Fishermen whispered strange and wonderful things about this cave ; and there it stood, grim and stark, in the wreathing mists of the morning, a dark patch open to the curling sea. One of Ifan's ancestors had had strange commerce in this cave ; and people wondered as to what manner of things happened in its murky depths. Some said that old Deio used to deal there with folk he should not have met, for he carried with him gifts of gold and silver from somewhere ; but no one knew whence. The story went on to say that Deio had for his wife, in that dark abode, a sea-maiden. That must be clear for anyone to guess. Otherwise there was no reason for his disappearance for weeks at a time and his possession of these gifts. But although fishermen often went to seek him they could never trace his whereabouts.

And by this cave sat our friend Ifan, for the times were hard, and a great desire had come upon him to enter the gloomy portals. For more than two years no wreck had come upon that coast. The outlook was very sad for the coming winter, and the mackerel and herring seemed to shun the shore. Up stood Ifan, and, with his mind all of

[1] Dio (short for David).

a tremble, he drew near to the mouth—that darksome, open mouth ! And then he came away ! Again he approached, wondering if he dared. The tide was running out, he was a good swimmer, and yet he could not enter.

" If the sea-maiden came to me," he said, as he sat down once more, " if she came, I should run for my life. And what would be the good of that ? Nothing whatever. I must clutch her, and beg her to marry me, or else I shall get no money. If I married her, then I should have wealth and all the money I could want, and that would be something worth having." Ifan scratched his head, and looked deep into the dark depths.

As he gazed, his eyes saw farther into the darkness and they caught sight of a candle that shed a pale, green light upon a narrow strip of sand which lay along a pool. By this pool sat a young girl combing her hair. Never had Ifan seen aught so lovely. Her fair skin was soft and shimmered like satin, and hair fell in silky, golden showers around her knees. Ifan went slowly towards her, and, as he approached, he heard her weeping bitterly and sighing sorely, while the glittering tears dropped from her eyelids like spring rain-drops sparkling from the sky. He put out his great, rough hand and gently stroked her soft, yielding hair in order to check her sorrow. Then he dared to touch her hand, but she uttered a scream like a savage thing caught in a net, and in spite of all his efforts to calm her, she grew more and more wild and timorous.

Ifan knew not what to do. That he was fortunate to be by the side of such a young and wealthy maiden he felt certain. But how could he win her consent to marriage so that he might get gold and silver wealth? In her hand she held her

" SHE UTTERED A SCREAM . . ."

golden comb, and around her fair neck hung a chain of gleaming pearls. Ifan's heart failed him; all he could do was to pat her hair as though she were one of his brother's children, that her fear might depart. At last he tried again to hold her white hand; but thereupon she screamed like half a dozen young screech owls, and Ifan heard afar off an answering cry.

" Go away," she cried ; " my brother is coming. Hasten ! but come to-morrow."

Then there leaped upon Ifan a spray which blinded him, and the pale flame of the green candle went out. Hither and thither was Ifan flung in the waters of the cavern. A rope passed over his head, and he bethought him to utter " Our Father," but there was no time amid the strife. Then in the twinkling of an eye, he was drawn without the cave, and though its sides were sharp with jutting rocks, and great blue stones lay under the surface of the water, yet he had no harm. The rope was still about him and lay around his waist, and, although he feared to touch it, he longed to draw it to him, for it would make a splendid cable for his boat. In spite of fear he dragged it from the sea. Lo ! at its other end he saw fastened a large trunk. He pulled eagerly, and, despite its heavy weight, still he tugged more strongly. But before he could pull it into the beach, behold, a mighty wave swelled up in the sea, and dragged him out of his depth ; then once again the sea leaped up, and a wave with a snowy crest lifted him on its bosom, and he found that he stood by the side of the trunk, upon a grassy mound, near the shore.

Who can tell of Ifan's joy when he saw the treasure nestling in the heart of that trunk ? Rings set with sparkling gems ; chains that glittered like the falling waters when they are scattered from the rock in the sunshine ; pearls as white as snow, and rubies red as fire—treasures without price lay before his wondering eyes. He hid them in haste, and, by night, he crept backwards and forwards till all was safe and sound in his cottage home. Then he went to bed and slept.

While yet a few pale stars twinkled faintly in the roseate sky, Ifan walked with a wondering mind towards the cave of Deio. Far he wandered in the faint and misty light, and ever his thought left him no peace. He wished now he had brought a torch to lighten the darkness of his mystic cave. And he trembled lest the treasure were the subtle creation of a dream woven in the sleep of the night. Long he waited in the cavern ; but no one came, and at last he made his way homeward, feeling that all was not real, and he had but dreamed a dream. Yet at home there lay the wondrous heap of jewels in their settings, so he placed them in skilful array in many a cunning corner, and, when the night had come, he sank again to sleep.

Then, in the darkness, a form came nigh unto him, and damp arms wrapped themselves around him. The more he strove to free himself, the closer grew the embrace, and he heard a whisper, faint as the breath of evening, speak the words, " Forget not to be early in the morn ! " " Stay ! " cried Ifan. " Wait till I get a light, and I will rise immediately." But before the words had left his

lips the visitor had gone ; there was nothing.
Ifan, rising in haste, searched for his treasure, and
he saw it by the candle light, gleaming and
glittering, gold and silver, gems and pearls, charms
and jewels without number.

Again the sun stole silently through the curtain
of the heavens, and Ifan set out for the shore,
while fear possessed him as he wandered by the
silvery sea. Yes, indeed, fear that never more
would his eyes look upon the little white house
with thatched roof, the home of his birth and
childhood. Then again his heart beat, and he
saw in his mind a vision of comfort and welfare.
As he mused he stood among his comrades by the
sea while they pulled their nets to the shore. It
was terrible to hear their language when the nets
came home ; for not a fish lay within the meshes,
and one man cried, " That curse of a sea-maiden
has opened our nets and set free the fish."

Ifan stole stealthily away, and then sped along
the shore. When he reached Deio's cave, whom
should he see at the entrance but the maiden
sleeking her hair with a golden comb. Yet to him
marvellous was the change which transformed her.
Before, she was but a slim girl ; now she stood
dressed richly like some great lady, and wearing
upon her head a crown of purest gold. As Ifan
approached she held out her fair hand, saying :

" Comest thou, Ifan ? I wish to dwell awhile
among the people of the land. Keep this," quoth

she, handing him a magic cap, " and I will wear a crown, for I am a king's daughter."

Ifan bent low before her, overcome by her wondrous beauty, and marvelling that she could be the same.

While yet the mists trembled in the embrace of the morning they two went their way, and Ifan was without speech, for he knew not what to say. He feared to mention his humble home, but even as this thought trod the pathways of his brain she knew of its existence. Turning to him, with a smile like the tender light which steals through the ivy into a darkened room, she said with a ripple of laughter in her voice :

" I know quite well that thou knowest not how to tell me of thy home. But think not of that, for I have long known thee, and seen thee oft, ever since, as a young lad with rosy cheek, thou didst fish from thy father's boat in the bay. In those days, I heard thee sing a song that won for thee the love of my heart. When I spake of thy song and sought to sing it to my father in his palace, all wondered at its music, and wished to hear it from end to end. So I came back often and listened for it, but in vain. Then was I permitted by those who love me to come seeking for thee with treasures, seeking that soul-melody which will not be taught save by treasure. Yet when I met thee I knew that wealth alone would not avail to win thee, but that I must appear as now thou seest me. My name is Nefyn [1] and I am the daughter to Nefydd-Naf-Neifion.[2] Nor am I without relations in thy world. Think then no more of thy cottage, but do as thou dost desire, and all shall be well."

Then Ifan asked her timidly if she would be his bride, and dwell with him for better or for worse? She answered that she was fain to do so, if he would teach her his song, nor let her see the magic cap. Then as the day grew brighter so more radiant seemed the face of his affianced bride, while Ifan's song came to him again, and he sang it to Nefyn :

> " Oh, feathered friend with pure blue wing,
>   Mild and obedient as a dove,
>   Now speed thee, speed thee to the maid
>   Who captured all my youthful love.
>   Yea, hasten, bird, and tell my sweet,
>   Tears stain my face,
>   They never tire.
>   For her embrace
>   I burn with fire—
>   Love lingers in my very pace.
>   Ah ! Beauty slaying me with love—
>   May God be gracious to such grace ! "

Yet their marriage was not easy, for the news spread abroad that Nefyn was a sea-maiden, and it was only by their wealth that all was settled. Then indeed they dwelt together in happiness, wandering hand in hand by the sea-shore, and often entering thus into the cave.

[1] Nevin.   [2] Nevith-Nav-Nivion, Nefydd Lord of Lords.

4

Time sped by and Ifan and Nefyn were as nobles in the land. Never was wife more tender and full of grace, nor husband more loving. There were born to them three sons and three daughters, and these children were beauteous as the young and slender flowers that grow in the meadows in the spring time.

One fine day when the sunlight dwelt upon the ocean and its rays were so strong that the young fish could be seen passing to and fro in the crystal depths, Ifan and Nefyn and their children went over the sea in a boat. Suddenly a storm sprang from the sky and the huge waves leapt to meet it. Through the tumult of air and water, screams and cries could be heard, and the children were sorely affrighted. Seeing their terror Nefyn bent over the side of the boat, and her moving lips showed that she was speaking to someone in the depths beneath. Great was the awe of the children at this, and they remembered the rumours that surrounded their mother's origin. Then Nefydd, the eldest son, thought of all he had heard from his parents of Nefydd-Naf-Neifion, and the valleys of Gwenhidiw,[1] and the country of Gwyn ab Nudd[2] (whose prince came to visit them), and his heart sank, for to him his mother was beautiful beyond compare, tenderest and kindest of all the world. Could she indeed be a sea-maiden from the unknown and mystic depths of the great grey sea?

[1] Gwenhidiū.   [2] Gwyn-ab-Nŭth.

One day there rode up to the home of Ifan a messenger, and, at night, when the crescent moon was sharp, pointed and pale in the western sky, Ifan and Nefyn departed, leaving the children in charge of a trusted servant. Then Nefydd, who watched them go, said to Eilonwy,[1] his sister, " Why should they set out by night ? " So they followed them along the shore. And lo ! a huge wave rose from out the glassy sea, and Nefyn, wrapping Ifan and herself in a cloak of skin, sank into the water's heart and passed from sight. At the sad knowledge of his mother's secret, the heart of Nefydd broke within him, and his sister, seeing that her brother was dead, no more desired to live, and flung herself into the sea.

As Eilonwy fell into the waves, a knight of beauteous form, and riding on a snow-white horse, came galloping swiftly over the waves, and bending low from the saddle caught the maiden in his arms, and bore her swiftly away.

In the house of Ifan all was confusion. Nefydd was dead, Eilonwy had cast herself away and could not be found. What could be done ? Then spake Tegid, the brave, handsome brother :

" If we get no message ere the morrow we must bury Nefydd in the waves, and perchance some of my mother's kinsfolk will come and fetch him."

But at midnight a knight came to the house and

[1] Eilònui.

"SANK INTO THE WATER'S HEART."

OWAIN OF DRWS COED

"They took Bela gently in their arms, and the air was full of sad farewells to Owain."

(Plate 3)

DAFYDD MEURIG

"Yet, as his fingers touched the gold his heart revived, and full soon he had filled the sack." *(Plate 4)*

bade them bury their brother as the early grey
dawn crept over the sea.

" Yet," said he, " do not mourn for Nefydd.
He shall come back to you and dwell with you once
more. And Eilonwy, the fair, lives as the bride of
the brightest and bravest knight of Gwerddonau-
Llion." [1]

At dawn, they bore the coffin out to sea, and lo !
as it sank into the cold waves, those who watched
saw Nefydd leave its shelter, and, with his arm
around the self-same messenger who bade them
hope, he passed into a ship which flew away with
them. Then of a truth, wonder reigned all over
the land as to what would happen thereafter.

Time sped by, and, when a year and a day had
passed, Ifan, royal in aspect and decked in regal
robes, came to his home. Nefyn did not return,
for she dwelt with her daughter for a time. All
was joy in the homestead, yet in the midst of the
joy came the dark stab of sorrow, for Ifan, in the
night which followed, sank into a death slumber,
and could not be awakened. Rumour told of a
black warrior who, in the night, stole silently to
the house and as silently departed.

On the morning of Ifan's burial Nefyn returned
to the sad home. Bitterly she wept, and in a brief
space she left the house again, and Tegid remained
as lord. Verily his lot was sad, and he needed all
his courage to face the dark looks of his neighbours.

[1] Gwerthonīthlion.

So threatening did they become that he sent his

" THE GLEAMING COILS OF A HUGE SERPENT."

sisters away to be educated elsewhere, and he and his brother remained to face the tumult.

One night the brothers dreamed the same dream. They saw, as it were, the black knight pass into Deio's cave. In the morning they went in haste to see if it were so, and before their very eyes the ship which brought their sisters home again was cast upon the rocky shore, and shattered. Yet they hastened to the cave, and here to their horror they beheld the gleaming coils of a huge serpent. As Tegid lifted his sword to strike, the serpent cried aloud :

" Strike me not, Tegid, for I am thy sister imprisoned by the black knight."

As she spoke the black knight came from a deep recess, and whirling his sword aloft struck off the serpent's head. But in vain. Another head came in its place, and, as it did so, a knight clad in white armour strode from another part. Then the sound of shrewd and awful blows resounded in Deio's cave. Full soon, however, the black knight lay dead in the dark cavern, and, as he died, Eilonwy sprang from the serpent's skin, and Nefyn rose from the waves and bore her children to their father's court—all, that is, except Tegid. He, loving his father dearly, remained for a year and a day by Ifan's grave, often consoled by Nefyn, who came to visit him. Great was his gladness when one day to the faithful lad came Ifan himself. After a long, fond embrace, Tegid, leaning on his loving father's arm, went joyfully to meet his kinsfolk at the Court of Nefydd.

IV

OWAIN OF DRWS COED [1]

UNTIL he reached the age of twenty no son could have been more devoted to his parents than Owain of Drws Coed. They loved him dearly, for he was their only child, and in return for their love Owain scarcely ever left his father and mother. As soon as he had finished the work of the farm, he would come in and join the old people, talk with them, and sing in a clear, musical voice many of the songs that they rejoiced to hear. He could play on the harp, and that made his song yet more delightful for those who listened.

Sometimes the people in the village, friends of the family at Drws Coed, would come to spend the evening, and Owain sang to them as well. They begged him to sing and play on the harp, for they said, " No one sings like Owain, and his harp is very sweet." And the maidens of the village looked shyly, yet with admiration, at Owain, for he was tall and straight as an arrow, and his eyes were deep and tender in their regard. Indeed,

[1] Druce Kōid, door of wood.

everyone loved Owain ; but Owain did not love everybody—only the dear old folk who lived in the ancient grey house of Drws Coed. So his boyhood slipped away, as the hours pass on a summer's morning, and lo ! Owain was twenty.

One day the mists came rolling down the mountain-sides like great puffs of breath from a giant's mouth. Vast ragged shreds they were as they left the mountain-top, and they came down to the valley as though the giant wished to hide the whole world from his view. Owain led his sheep lower down the slope, because the mist had laid thousands of sparkling drops upon the grass, and moss-covered rocks, and also on the backs of the sheep ; and there was no blue sky to be seen anywhere. He wished to find a sheltered spot in the well-known valley where the flock could be safely shut in a pen. As he drove them before him he reached Cwm Marchnad,[1] where the reeds grow tall and rich, and the ground is always marshy. Owain little thought what was awaiting him in this place ; but he went on, driving his sheep before him, and thinking of the old folk at home.

Then, all at once, his eyes beheld under the shelter of a large, grassy mound a figure which made his heart throb and leap within him. It was a young and exceedingly beautiful girl. Never had Owain dreamed that such beauty could be

[1] Koom Marchnad, valley of the market.

upon our earth ; for this lass as much surpassed the gentle maids of the village as the delicate, winning wild-rose surpassed the wool flowers his mother worked into her patterns. He could only stand and stare at her with all his might, as though he wished his eyes could drink in all her beauty.

Her hair was very long, and lay about her in curling masses of fine golden threads. So very golden was it that it seemed to have caught some of the rays of the hidden sun. Her eyes were as blue and sparkling as the summer skies, and her forehead was as white as the foam that dwells on the leaping wave, or as the snow new fallen from heaven. Her face was rounded with the fresh beauty of youth, and her cheek blushed like the red roses of summer, and as Owain looked at her lips, which were small and perfectly shaped, and rich in colour, he thought they were so pretty that even an angel would desire to kiss them. Yet Owain had never before had the thought of love in his heart, and he loved best of all to sing and play the harp to the old people at Drws Coed. But now love had surged through his veins as the rich light of the early summer floods the fields of young corn, and ripens them to harvest. He was heartstricken ; yea, he who was so timid and shy drew near to the wondrous girl, as pieces of paper fly towards amber. In faltering words, and speaking rather with his eyes than with his voice, he asked her whether he might stay and converse with her. She smiled courteously upon him, and, reaching forth a hand pure white as the drooping

"HER HAIR . . . LAY ABOUT HER IN CURLING MASSES."

snowdrop, took his rough, red hand and said, " Idol of my hopes, thou hast come at last ! "

Then Owain's tongue lost its fear, and the words flowed smoothly as the brook which has reached the valley. He spoke of love and the springtide, of his father and mother at home, and the old grey farm of Drws Coed ; and the maiden sat and listened with her gentle hands folded in her lap, and her eyes, tender and sweet, watching his lips as they formed the words and disclosed his white teeth. Ever and anon she smiled at his beauty, as he marvelled at hers ; and so the hours slipped swiftly away.

Not far away along the valley was the Llyn y Gadair,[1] a lake that lay all shut in by the protecting mountains. Here there was perfect peace, silence like the silence of Heaven, and the beauty of nature at her sweetest and best. Around the silvery margin of the lake stood young groves of birch-trees, whose white barks were flaky with the swelling wood, and beyond these groves lay fields which were clothed in the spring with the purity of the daisy and the gleam of the golden buttercup. Hither Owain and Bela would wander, hand in hand, speechless, yet by their glances telling more than words could express, and forgetful of the worlds above and below.

At last, Love so much overcame Owain that he was restless day and night when Bela was absent from him. Sometimes, ere yet it was dawn, he would arise and sing :

[1] Llin e gadair, lake of the chair.

" O sweeter to me is the face of my Fair,
    More beautiful far than the rose ;
More golden than sunshine the strands of her hair,
    When day draweth near to a close.

Like fire in the heart is my Love, when 'tis day,
    And Love filleth my soul in the night.
Then hearing these words, Love, O do not delay,
    But come with thy glances so bright."

And Owain's father and mother and his many
friends thought the black-haired boy was be-
witched, for thus he sang in the night, while by
day he would wander away for long spells, and
no one could tell whither he had gone, nor what
had become of him.

But at length the secret lay open, and all knew
of Owain's love. Yet before Owain told his story
he and Bela had passed through a long and loving
courtship by the Llyn y Gadair. For thither
would Owain turn his steps, and there was Bela
always awaiting him. For this reason the place
of their tryst has been known as the Maiden's
Bower, and in this sacred haunt the young lovers
spent the golden hours of youth, and determined,
as time went on, to marry.

But if they were to marry it was necessary for
Bela to obtain her father's consent, and who could
tell how he would view her love for Owain ? Yet
she told him ; and the word came to Owain to
await her father in the woods. Accordingly, on
the night when the full moon floated in the sky,

Owain went out and waited to hear his fate, and stood long and anxiously among the silver birches, while nature slept, and the moonlight danced on the ripples of Llyn y Gadair.

For a long time there was no sign of living person other than himself ; but as the moon passed over and beyond the mountain-side, there came towards him two forms. By the soft misty hair Owain recognized the beautiful Bela. Her head bent low as she drew near to her lover. The other form was that of an old man, with a kindly peaceful face and silver-streaming hair. He came gently up to Owain, and taking the lad's hand placed within it the white hand of Bela. Then he said :

" Thou shalt have my daughter, Owain, but on one condition only. Never shalt thou allow cold iron to touch her flesh. If thou dost, then she shall no longer be thine, but shall return at once to her own people."

Then Owain was blithe at heart, and his voice was as the flow of the nightingale's song when all the woods are hushed to hear it sing its lay of love. Gladly he consented to the condition. There was no talk about any dowry, for love was the only acceptable one. Then the silver-haired old father led away the shy and lovely Bela. Yet before they departed, Owain and she had fixed the day for their marriage.

On the appointed day they were married, and all those present at the ceremony declared that they

"THE OTHER FORM WAS THAT OF AN OLD MAN."

had never seen at the altar a more handsome or fairer couple. People tell how a large sum of money came with Bela as her dowry ; for the people of Tylwyth Têg are as wealthy as those who dwell among the hills of gold, and on the wedding night the charming virgin went to Drws Coed, rich in the golden offerings of her kinsfolk. And very soon after that the young master shepherd of Cwm Marchnad was a rich and responsible man.

After the fashion of nature, in due time children were born to Owain and Bela, and they and their family lived happily together. Everything passed in sweet contentment for many a year. Yes, indeed, wealth poured in continually, for Fortune is a wondrous dame. She is the eldest daughter of Providence, and to her, as to her mother, are entrusted marvellous treasures to impart them as she is disposed. The old proverb says that water runs down to the valley, and so it was with this couple. They became wealthy beyond the average lot of man.

But the fair rose hath her sting ; night will ever follow day. One cannot have the sweet without the bitter, and even so it came to pass for Owain and Bela.

One day the husband and wife chanced to ride out and visit the cherished margin of Llyn y Gadair. As they rode, Bela went too near the water, and, its foot slipping, her horse sank into the water up to its girth. Owain hastened to save his dear wife, and, when the horse was safely on shore again, he helped Bela to get off her wet steed and mount his own. Alack the day ! in his hurry

" CHANCED TO RIDE OUT."

to place her little foot in the stirrup, the iron slipped and just touched her knee. They looked at one another with faces pale as the mistletoe-berry, and hastened to gallop home.

5

Ere they had reached half way, there stole down the hill-side the strains of sweetest music. Rippling and entrancingly it came, wreathing and folding in its gentle murmurs and tender cadences everything around the mountain foot. And, as the harmonies sank into Owain's soul, he saw that they were surrounded with a myriad of the " small people," while others came rushing down the hill-side. They looked at him, and the tears stole down from their eyes. They took Bela gently in their arms and the air was full of sad farewells to Owain. Then as the mist comes suddenly and obscures the view, so Owain stood looking at the empty saddle of his dear wife's horse. Bela, his beautiful, loving Bela, had passed away before his sight, and he knew not where to seek her.

Some people in the district say that she was taken to the Maiden's Bower, and thence to the land of Hud, that she left her dear little ones to the care of her beloved, and that she came no more to their presence. But there are others who speak with more confidence and narrate a happier story, for they tell how every now and again Owain and his little ones would catch a glimpse of the lovely Bela. And it happened in this wise. Since the laws of her country forbade her to tread the earth with any human being, as she had been touched with iron, she and her mother thought long and earnestly, and at last they contrived a way in which she could see and converse with her husband and

children once again. They obtained a large turf—
great enough to float and at the same time support
Bela. This they were wont to place on the surface
of the lake not far from the silver strand, and here
she would sit almost within reach of her dear ones,
and for long, sweet hours hold loving talk with
them. Thus they all lived together till time
loosened Owain's soul, and it passed away on the
breeze of the morning.

V

LLYN TEGID

OR

THE STORY OF BALA LAKE

THERE are many wonders in the depths of the sea, wonders of coral, and sea-weed, and sea-fish, great and small. Much treasure is buried in those great silent depths, and a world of which we know very little is always lying there hidden from the eye of man. For man requires the light of the pleasant sun and keep draughts of glorious air to breathe, and in those darksome depths sun and air are absent. There is the throne of the realm of the waters, and what mighty sovereign holds sway from that throne no man can say or imagine.

Great lakes have also their mysterious, silent depths. As they lie in the heart of the mountains, these lakes flash and sparkle, where the sun shines on them, like great fields of precious stones, and, when the sky is grey, they look as threatening as a giant's frown. But that is only their surface. What lies down there, in the depths below, where all is silent and hidden? Who would dare to plunge into those depths, some moonlight night when the silvery light is running to and fro over the waves like the foot-prints of fairies, and sink ever deeper and deeper, right down to the lowest depths ? What would such a bold diver see if he reached that vast and sombre kingdom ? Ah ! what indeed. Yet there are strange stories about those unknown regions ; stories which carry one back into the past years of the rolling world, when life which we have never known sported and gloomed with the rapid beat of Time. Do you wish to hear the echo of its vanished greatness ? Then you must go and stand near some wide surface when all nature is lying in deep repose and listen for the music that has left the world.

Sometimes, when one is listening intently, there comes as from a fairy world the silvery sound of the pealing of distant bells. It rises and falls faintly upon the peaceful air, then passes into silence. Perhaps it is some chime from the mystic depths calling low and sweet for the evensong. Now it will come with mirth and joyance, as if wedding bells were pealing for a hidden world to rejoice in the plighting of two faithful hearts—or is it the voice of victory over some vanquished foe that steals over the rippling waves ? Once again it comes, this time soft and slow, mournfully, sadly, touching some regretful memory in the heart, for it is the passing bell tolling for a soul that has winged its flight ; and the mourners pass in dark garb to the open grave in the hill-side.

Some people say that when water and air are both at perfect rest (a thing that happens on very rare occasions) one can see, down in the stilly depths, wonderful sights which reveal themselves. For magnificent cities spring into being, lifting high in their watery envelopment the glorious summits of their trees and spires. Rare and costly buildings, fashioned from marble of wondrous hues, stand there in their majestic splendour. Through the heart of those cities of the depths run broad roads, lined with many a fair mansion ; here and there squares and gardens break the masses of architecture with green spaces, and waving branch and frond. Factories and work-shops, wharves and market places tell of the former rush of life, while without the walls lie broad tracts of pure white sand, marked with oases of shells and weed—a wilderness of peace around strange abodes of silence. Then, with a shiver and sudden shadowing, the waters cover up the vision and the human eye can see no more.

Once upon a time there was a powerful prince whose rule extended far and wide over mountains and vales. He was the mighty owner of forest and field, tilth and pasture. Rich mines poured their wealth into his coffers ; the orchards and the harvests shook their ruddy and golden wealth into his barns and storehouses ; the peasant paid to

him his humble tribute of human toil with the
sweat of his brow. If such a prince, with such
possessions, had been kind and wise the valleys
might have shouted for joy, and the mountains
have lifted their summits to repeat their song of
praise to the blue heavens above. But, far from
being wise and kind, the heart of this prince was
bitter and wickedly cruel, so that wherever he rode
men shrank from meeting him. He ruled his
territory with a rod of iron and a hand of cunning,
fierce oppression. When he was a young man,
men dreaded him ; in his age they trembled afar
off at the very thought of his malignant spirit.
The neighbourhood teemed with the tales of his
evil, and there was none to say him nay ; no, not
one. Men hardly dared whisper, " Beware of
Tegid the Bald," lest the breeze should carry the
whisper to his ears, so quick was he to know the
spoken word. The common people said that the
very stones had ears, and carried news to Tegid.

So he lived his life, and at first nothing disturbed
him in his wicked ways. He began to build a
stately palace, for his power was regal, and he
forced men to toil day and night at the labour of
quarrying and fashioning huge blocks of marble
to form the massive walls. For years masons,
carpenters, and joiners gave constant and painful
service to the decoration of many a lofty hall, and,
when the work was near completion, forest and
field were cleared to make way for the most

wondrous garden that the eye of man had ever beheld. Yet this work was built with his peasants' life blood, and Tegid laughed to see them toiling, from dewy morn till the sinking of the sun.

"Fools and knaves!" he cried, "cease your work for but one moment, and the lash shall sting you into energy," and they cowered at the violent looks in the bloodshot eyes turned upon them.

Thus the work went on. Year by year Tegid's wealth increased, and year by year his peasants moaned, toiled, died, and were forgotten. Even so in life at this time we see men take the golden fruit they have not earned. Yes, and they laugh in their shallow ignorance, thinking that they have more wealth than their fellow-men, and then, in their foolish chatter to their friends, tell how poor creatures toil that they may grow rich. Yet over all their vain boasting there bends a listening ear. Not one word of such wicked vaunting ever escapes that ear, and, in due course, sooner or later, seen or unseen, comes a curse which eats like a canker-worm. This thing is true, let men doubt it if they will.

Tegid might have known this, if he had cared to heed the warning that was sent to him ; but he turned deaf ears, and laughed at the thought of changing his evil ways, till his sides shook. Sometimes he grew angry at the voice of warning, yet he could not check it, or in any way prevent the notes falling upon his ears, for they came from a little bird that was so quick in its movements that it was gone before the message had fallen from its little throat. " Vengeance will come ! Vengeance will come ! " was the burden of its tiny song. This was the only hindrance in Tegid's way. And what a poor hindrance it was ! He felt no remorse, but moved in vicious hatred because he could not quiet this feeble fore-warning of the evil that shall befall all wrong-doers. " Curse the bird ! " he exclaimed, and went away to lash and ill-treat his hard-worked people.

In time the palace was finished, and the eldest daughter of Tegid was of marriageable age. She was a true daughter of her wicked father, and her hand was given to a mighty lord who lived beyond the mountains. Indeed, there was not one of the family of Tegid the Bald who was lovely and of good report. Evil they were born, and evilly they lived, ever waxing more and more vile and base as the days wore on and they grew like unto their sire. But the day of the wedding drew nigh, and Tegid the Bald resolved to celebrate the event by throwing open his stately palace and the beautiful grounds that seemed like fairy-land.

Thus he sent invitations far and wide to his friends, and when the day dawned there were gathered together all Tegid's kith and kin, all his friends and companions, all those who had joined in, or laughed at, the ways of this wicked man. All were there; not one was missing.

In the early morning Tegid went abroad to cast a keen eye on the preparations for the events of the noble day. With cutting word and heavy hand he passed upon his way, and, as he walked along, a tiny voice overhead piped " Vengeance will come ! Vengeance will come ! " With an evil curse Tegid glanced upward and saw the tiny bird flutter from twig to twig, and again came the warning sound. Then the remembrance of the winged messenger passed from Tegid's mind while he was in fierce heat over a servant's neglect, and afterwards he plunged headlong into mirth and merriment. The wine-bowl passed from mouth to mouth; the strains of lovely music passed richly through the palace rooms and stole without, bathing flowers and fruit in their melody; while overhead the warm sun passed on its daily journey, glancing with seeming indifference upon the glittering display of man's magnificence. Away on the hill-side the peasants gloried in at least a few hours' respite from the sting and fury of Tegid's evil nature.

Noontide came and passed away; afternoon, with its soft languor, yielded to golden eventide; and the even with its brief, soft light bowed low and sank into the silvery calm of the early night.

An old and toil-worn harper was threading his way through the lonely world. As he passed along the village street he asked a woman at a cottage door if there were any mansions nearby where he might get some food and shelter for the night. She looked at him gravely, and often casting her eyes about to see that none was listening, she whispered, " Go away, old harper, as soon as you may. This

" LOVELY LADIES . . . PASSED LAUGHING ON THEIR WAY."

place is evil and there is no reward here save that of the whip and cruel word, or, perchance, even worse. Go speedily away ! " Then she turned and went within. The poor old man knew that he must eat or die, and failing to get sustenance at the village, he came at length to the palace grounds, and heard the sound of music and dancing.

Such a scene met his faded old eyes as he had never beheld before. The moonlight poured down upon the giant outlines of the palace and silvered it with many a glimmering line of trembling light. The windows glowed with the warm hue of lamp and candle light ; and shrub and tree, sparkling with pendent decorations, seemed each a little star-set firmament, so many were the lights that shone for the guidance of the dancers. Brave lords and lovely ladies, clothed in silks and satins of many a dazzling tint, passed laughing on their way, or moved in stately measures to the strain of the music that streamed from the banqueting hall.

The soul of the harper revived as he heard the lilt of the music, and in response he took up his harp, and played. A servant brought him food and wine. Then he played again. As his fingers wandered tenderly over the strings while he sat among the trees, he heard a note sound overheard, and, looking up, he saw a little bird, with ruffled plumage, moving from twig to twig ; and as he looked he loved it. The little creature bent its head to one side and sang its monotonous song, " Vengeance, vengeance ! "

It seemed to the old man that the tiny creature was beckoning him to follow. So he arose, and moved towards it ; and again the bird uttered its warning and travelled still further, while the aged

" HE SAW A LITTLE BIRD."

harper followed. If for a moment he stopped, the

note became more insistent, and seemed even sorrowful and heart-breaking. So they went on, and at last the harper stood at the top of a lofty hill far away from the gay palace, far away from the merry music, where he was alone with the bird. And now he felt his fatigue come again, so, laying his harp upon the ground, he kissed it, bidding it good-night, according to his custom. He sank down to welcome peaceful slumber, broken only by the murmurs of a babbling brook. Yet before he could sleep there shot into his remembrance the taste of the food and wine, and the shimmer of the glories he had so easily abandoned. Then he arose, and eagerly sought the downward path. But he could not find it again. In vain he wandered on the hill-side in the endeavour to return, till at last, perforce, he had to lie down and sleep.

When he awoke his eyes were turned towards the valley of Tegid the Bald. He was amazed at what he beheld, and rubbed his eyes to make sure that he dwelt in the land of reality, and was not a traveller in the realm of sleep. No, indeed, he was wide awake, and what he saw was the accomplishment of the foretelling of the tiny messenger. Below him lay the wide, smooth surface of a lake. So calm it looked as it reflected the morning light that one might have supposed it had been there for ever. But the harper knew that this was not so. In the short hours of one

calm, summer night the water had swallowed
up the evil years of the life of Tegid the

" BELOW HIM LAY THE . . . SMOOTH SURFACE OF A LAKE."

Bald, and all the wearisome labour that he had
enforced.

So lies Bala Lake, over the scene of iniquity,

and the Palace of Tegid is fanned no more by the soft airs of the day ; yet, once upon a time, when a boatman was plying his oars one moonlight night, he ceased to row and let his craft drift on into stillness and silence. Then as he gazed into the waters, he plainly saw the massive towers and glint of the marble walls, while a faint cadence reached his ears, the sound, as it were, of the tiny bird piping its sad message, " Vengeance will come ! Vengeance will come ! "

VI

DAFYDD MEURIG OF BETWS BLEDRWS [1]

A LEGEND OF KING ARTHUR

DAFYDD was not always a willing boy. Indeed, he must have been very trying at times to his parents ; but they were very patient and would never have driven him away from the farmhouse at Betws Bledrws. No, Dafydd left home of his own accord. And it happened in this way.

Owen Meurig, his father, went out one morning very early in order to lead the flock to fresh pastures. Dafydd ought to have been up early enough to accompany his father ; but Owen said, " I cannot wait for the lazy fellow, and I haven't time to go and pull him out of bed. Send him after me directly he comes down ! " Then he went off to lead the sheep.

Some time afterwards down came Dafydd yawning like a dog.

" Where's my breakfast ? " he asked.

" No breakfast for you, my son, this morning," said the mother. " If you cannot get down soon

[1] Dafith Murig of Bettūs Bledrūs.

6

enough to help your father with the sheep you must march on an empty stomach."

Then all Dafydd's sleepiness disappeared. Anger took its place instantly.

" If you don't let me have breakfast," he shouted, " I'll run away and never come home any more ! "

Now his mother thought he was speaking louder than his intention, so she answered very quietly :

" Good-bye, Dafydd, I hope you'll be in a better temper when you do come back."

Dafydd walked out of his home without another word.

When his father returned at night there was no Dafydd to be seen ; although the neighbourhood was searched high and low, yet the lad was not discovered anywhere. He had completely disappeared, and we must follow him on his travels to see what strange adventures fell to his share.

Dafydd, in spite of all his laziness and wilful ways, was not a bad boy at heart. He had some very good points, and one of these was a desire to find out a reason for everything. He also wanted to know more of the world, and for some time it had been his intention to ask his parents to let him go out and earn his living elsewhere. But very foolishly he kept his longing silent in his heart and never said a word to his father and mother, who were very kind people and would have done all they could to humour the wayward lad. So

Dafydd had gone on day by day with his desire swelling in his heart like a kernel in a husk, and now in this cruel manner he ran away from home.

As he tramped on he felt more and more sorry, yet more resolved not to go home and eat humble pie. " I'll go to London," said he to himself, " and see that wonderful bridge that people talk about so much." So he cut himself a staff from a hazel-tree on a hill-side, and on he went. Yet before Dafydd got to London he had found the world a very different place from what he had imagined it to be in his home in Wales. He soon saw how good his parents had been to him. He had to work hard to earn a crust ; and there was no more late sleep in the morning. If he had not had a brave heart, Dafydd would have turned home again. But no ; he had resolved to go to London, and there he at last arrived.

Dafydd lived in London for several years, but his heart ever turned towards home. This was especially so on Sunday, when he was free from hard work, and had leisure to walk about and think. He often remembered the old folk, the pleasant farm on the green hill-side, and the wide backs of the grim, old mountains standing in silence here and there. When he was very lonely he went to that wonderful bridge, not nearly so wonderful as people had made out, yet quite wonderful enough to interest Dafydd ; for he loved to watch the water rushing by the pillars, and to see the boats

and ships coming and going on the broad breast
of the river.

One day, as he leaned over the parapet watching
the busy scenes, a voice said in his ear :

" Whence do you come, young friend ? "

Dafydd turned and saw an Englishman looking
at him with quizzical eyes, and so he replied
somewhat sullenly :

" I come from my own country."

" Quite so," replied the other ; " but do not be
vexed with me, and answer my questions frankly,
for if you do, you will not be sorry."

" Well," said Dafydd, " what do you want to
know ? "

" Where did you get that hazel stick ? " asked
the stranger.

Dafydd told him he had cut it from a tree by
the road-side not far from his home at Betws.

" Can you remember the exact spot ? " asked
the Englishman.

" Yes," said Dafydd, " I can."

" Then, my friend, your fortune is made ; for
that stick in your hand grew on a spot under which
are hidden treasures of gold and silver. If you
do indeed remember the place, and can conduct
me to it, I will put you in the way of being the
richest man in Wales."

Dafydd looked his man straight in the face. He
had lived long enough in London to know that he
could not trust everybody, and he wondered

whether this stranger was trying to deceive him ; but no, his eyes were frank and open, and Dafydd guessed that he was one of those who know many hidden secrets, who can read the stars, and who know where the water flows in the depths of the earth. So he said, " Let us go now, then, at once, and I will show you where I cut this stick."

Therefore Dafydd and the stranger journeyed together down to Wales, to the old hazel-tree growing by the road-side.

It was night time when they came along the road leading to Betws, and the twinkling stars dotted the deep blue sky as white anemones tremble in the midst of blue-bells in the woods when spring sings over the hill-side. The old hazel-tree grew at the foot of a rocky mass called Craig-y-Ddinas,[1] and in the darkness it looked like some gaunt old creature of the hills leaning in anger across the road, with its arms above its head ready to strike.

" This is the tree," said Dafydd.

" Well, then, here we must dig," replied his companion ; and they set to work with a will, digging under the spreading roots of the gnarled hazel-tree.

Soon they struck upon something hard under the soil. It was a broad, flat stone, and when they raised it they saw that it had covered a passage which led deep down into the hill-side. Dafydd

[1] Kraig er thinas.

now thrilled with excitement, and his comrade also was nearly as excited as he.

" Are you afraid to come down with me ? " he asked.

" Not I," answered Dafydd, and down they went in the gloomy depths.

Then, as they proceeded in dread, they became aware that their feet were treading on well-carved, stone steps, and gradually light appeared from great lamps hung in the rocky roof overhead. They went on and on, along the well-lit stone passage, green with age, and lo ! to Dafydd's surprise they came to a huge silver bell that hung low on a silver chain from the rocks above. The Englishman paused and touched Dafydd's arm.

" Tread carefully to one side," said he, " and on no account touch that bell, or you will have reason to be sorry."

So they passed very carefully, and soon the passage led them to an enormous cave, which opened out like a well-built hall in the very heart of Craig-y-Ddinas. Overhead, and around the walls, flashed hundreds of lamps of massy silver, and their rays fell on a sight such as man had surely never seen before.

All about the floor of this spacious hall lay the figures of mighty warriors fully clothed in perfect armour, and each warrior was in deep repose. That they were not dead but merely sleeping Dafydd could easily see by the rising and falling of their broad chests, and by the movement of their beards as the breath of their nostrils passed over them.

" ALL ABOUT . . . LAY MIGHTY WARRIORS."

Each man was of giant build, and their arms, bare to the elbow, looked hard and tough as steel. The light fell on breastplate and hauberk, lance and buckler, helm and corselet, so that armour and weapons glinted in the rays. Away in the far distance stood a table, round and fashioned from marble of rich and varied vein. Seated about

" HE SAT IN AN OLD-FASHIONED CHAIR."

this table were thirty-and-one mighty forms of men. Yet of their number there was one of far mightier mould than the others. He sat in an old-fashioned chair, with his head resting on his

left hand. On the table just before him lay a
sword that looked like a gleam of lightning, so
brilliantly it flashed, and at his side stood a shield
as massive as an oaken door. Near him lay a
huge hound. The warrior sat thus in majesty,
with his long, silvery beard sweeping the table,
while his large right hand lay like a thunderbolt
before him. Near it rested a crown of gold set
with many a gleaming gem. His eyes were
closed. Dafydd was fain to look away lest those
lids should open and the awful eyes flash their
stern light upon him. But silence, as of death
itself, lay upon everything.

In the midst of this hall stood two large heaps,
one of gold and the other of silver, and the
stranger whispered cunningly to Dafydd that he
might take what he would from the one or the
other, but not from both the heaps. In trembling
haste the youth obeyed. Yet his companion did
not so much as touch a coin, for he murmured
something about knowledge being better than
riches, and stood and looked with a curious eye
upon the scene. When Dafydd had laden himself
so that he could not carry another piece of gold,
they stepped noiselessly from that hall of sleep, and
reached the passage. Again the stranger warned
Dafydd not to touch the bell ; and so they passed
into the open air, and stood beneath the clear sky.

The grey dawn was just showing the dim outlines of the mountains as the two parted, Dafydd

to go to his home, and the stranger—no one can tell whither. Yet, before they separated, they replaced the stone and the earth beneath the roots of the hazel-tree.

Then the man said :

" You may perchance use your gold with lack of wisdom, although with prudence you have abundance, nay, more than enough for a lifetime. Be wise and go not again to the cavern. Yet, should you go, remember this : That bell stands waiting, waiting ever to call the mighty King Arthur and his knights and warriors to drive the Saxons from the land, what time the Cymry [1] are in need of their services. If you should chance to rouse the awful clamour of the bell, the whole host would rise, and with a shout fit to shake Craig-y-Ddinas, would cry, ' IS IT DAY ? ' Then you must reply at once, ' No ! it is not day, sleep on.' Thus only will you escape unscathed. For they sleep till the hour when the Black Eagle and the Golden Eagle shall go to war, and the loud tones of the silver bell shall cause the earth to tremble and their hosts to pour forth to re-possess the Isle of Britain."

Great was the joy at Betws Bledrws when Dafydd returned to the old people. He told them of his life and fortune, and, as he was now wise and old enough to settle down to his occupation, he lived quite happily in the old farmhouse.

[1] Kimrĕ, the Welsh.

As time went on he married, and his children gladdened the fields with their merry shouts. Yet Dafydd would often stand and look far away to where Craig-y-Ddinas rose gaunt and craggy against the sky. He thought of what lay beneath that rocky mass, and of the sleep of silence in the spacious hall. Then, at times, a voice would say, " Go and fetch more gold ! " Yet he did not dare, so awesome was the remembrance of those slumbering warriors, and of that mighty majesty seated in the carven chair.

The years passed on, and ever and again the voice spoke in Dafydd's ear, till at last, one evening taking mattock and a sack, he stole away, saying nothing of his intention to anyone. As soon as night fell he set to work. There sure enough was the broad, flat stone, and beneath it the open passage-way to the mighty hall. His heart failed him, yet he looked at the sack and pressed forward. Light again stole mysteriously on his sight, lighting a pathway to the silver bell. There it hung ! He crept by with nervous care so that he should not so much as let his breath fall upon it. Once again he stood in the midst of those mighty warrior forms, this time the only wakeful person there, and he trembled violently as he drew near to the golden pile. Yet, as his fingers touched the gold his heart revived, and full soon he had filled the sack, yes, filled it to the utmost, so that he could not close it, but had to grip one side of the mouth with both hands as he carried it over his shoulder.

Thus he staggered out with haste, never glancing backwards till he reached the passage. Then, indeed, his breath came again, and he went on with less fear. Alas, for Dafydd! As he reached the bell, he stepped heedfully aside lest he should touch its silver walls. He himself did not touch it, nor did his sack, but one heavy golden piece tumbled sideways from the sack, and fell upon the awful bell!

One long, silvery note swept up and down the passage, as though an archangel had touched a string of his harp with warning hand.

Forthwith there was a stir and a bustle, and a murmur as of a rising tempest. From iron throats came the mighty cry :

"Is it day? Is it day?"

Iron-shod feet came thundering upon the stone floor of the passage. So they rushed, thronging in haste and eager, to where the miserable Dafydd stood tongue-tied and forgetful of all, save his horror, as the sweat dropped from his white face. They came and stood towering around him, mighty warriors, angry, and roused from sleep. Their flashing eyes lit upon the sack as it lay mouthing out its contents beneath the silver bell; and then they knew.

"Slay the caitiff!" quoth one.

But a voice, as it were of the silver bell itself, came through the pent air of the passage :

" Slay him not ! " and Dafydd's eyes turned to where that awful form stood like some peerless headland above a raging storm. " Slay him not, but cast him out. For it is not yet day, and we

" THEY CAME AND STOOD . . . AROUND HIM."

must sleep long in our slumbers. Nevertheless, close the entrance that we be not again awakened till that dawn appears."

Then King Arthur turned and passed again into the hall, and the sword Excalibur gleamed in the darkness as the lightning flashes across a stormy sky.

So they led Dafydd to the entrance. Yet, ere they cast him out, one giant warrior struck him a blow that crushed him like the fall of a huge oak-

"STRUCK HIM A BLOW."

tree. Dazed and bruised he lay without, while the stone was drawn back to its resting-place.

As long as Dafydd lived he was a cripple. It is said that when the news of his disaster spread abroad, people went to discover the Hall of Slumber in Craig-y-Ddinas, but though their search was thorough they could not discover the entrance to that resting-place. And so King Arthur sleeps undisturbed till the Cymry are in straits, and the great bell once more rings its silvery warning in the silence of the passage.

VII

ELFOD THE PRIEST

EVERYBODY knew Elfod the Priest and everybody loved him very much. He was such a fine-looking old man. His hair was so silvery and long, his eyes so dark and tender, and his smile so winsome. No one could ever remember Elfod saying an angry word, except when Idris Vychan threw a sharp stone and cut an old woman's head. Then Elfod's eyes looked like live coals, instead of deep lakes under the clear open sky. If a child had some tiny trouble it would run straight to Elfod and tell him all about it, and, before long, one might see Elfod and the little one walking hand in hand quite happily, and all the trouble was forgotten.

The priest lived in an old stone house at the very end of the village, just where the mountain came down to meet the valley. In front of his house a noisy streamlet played all day long among the round stones that tried to prevent it from passing Elfod's door. They could never keep the stream quiet, and no one could ever make Elfod rest. He was always going about seeking to make other people happy.

No one else dwelt in the old, grey house. Elfod lived very simply on fruit and berries, and drank water from the laughing stream. Sometimes

" WALKING HAND IN HAND."

people would put on Elfod's doorstep something nice to eat, and then run out of sight before he could see who it was. Usually, about ten minutes later, some poor man or woman in the village would receive a visit from Elfod and a present of whatever had been left on the priest's doorstep.

7

Now the time drew near when Elfod felt that he was growing old, so old that he soon must go away to the angels, and he bethought him that no one knew anything at all about his early life. People had often said to him " Where did you live when you were a boy ? " or, " Who were your father and mother ? " or, perhaps, some wee child asked, " Who made you so kind and good ? " When such questions were asked the dark eyes seemed clouded with tender memory, the gentle mouth had a sad line on each side of it, and once a little girl had seen two big tears run down the wrinkles on Elfod's face. So generally people did not like to ask such questions, for they loved above all to see him smile. And now Elfod felt that he ought to tell someone about his early days before he left the village, the old grey house, the chatter of the stream, and went away to live elsewhere. So he called together several of his dearest friends, and they sat down under some oak-trees which grew in the valley, and Elfod spoke to them as follows :

" My mother's name was Gwenllian, and I was born long long ago—I do not know how long— in the village past the monastery, on the other side of the mountain. My parents were very good to me, and somewhat spoiled their little boy, for I was the only child in the family. With great sorrow I confess that I did not return their love as I should have done ; but thought simply of my own feelings and did what pleased myself. My father owned some sheep, and each day he would lead them forth to pasture on a mountain slope, or in the valley, according to the time of year. Very often as I grew older he would take me with him ; and, at first, great was my pleasure to lie and see the tiny white clouds run like sheep across the great blue field of the sky, or watch the sunlight chase the shadows over the slopes and along the rounded backs of the old grey mountains. Best of all I loved the early summer, when the broom blossomed yellow-gold over the earth, and the grass grew rich and green, luscious for the sheep to browse, and restful for the eye to behold. I loved the swift flight of the eagle, yet I feared his swoop upon the valley. From one spot I could see the misty blue of the distant sea lying between two rugged old mountains. I rejoiced to see the seasons' colours spread over the world, and hear the wind whisper as it passed by on some busy message.

" As I grew older I became restless, and then I lay no longer by my father's side, but wandered off alone to find things strange and new. ' Who can tell,' thought I, ' but that some day I may chance to discover the land of Hud-a-Lledrith ? ' [1] And so it befell, although, to be sure, I never really thought that such would be my fortune.

" One day, when I was about twelve or thirteen

[1] Hid-a-llédrith, charm.

years old, and had grown thoroughly tired of looking after my father's flock in the valley, I left the sheep and entered into a wood of oak, and ash, and thorn trees, and so wilful was I, so heedless of my parents' love, that I strayed alone in that wood for two days and two nights without taking even a morsel of food. As I roamed about the wood there came to me two mannikins, each about three feet high, and one said to me, very courteously and gently, ' Come with us, Elfod, and thou shalt obtain all that thy heart desires.' My heart beat fast, and even seemed to dance, as I answered that I would indeed go with them and that I rejoiced to do so. Then I followed after them, and we went towards the mountain-side till we reached a fair, broad field. I cannot tell you how it was, but, at a certain spot, my mannikins sank down through the sward, and with their merry eyes fixed on mine I was able to follow mirthfully. Nor was it long before we came to rest in a land glorious beyond compare, and as strange as it was beautiful.

" We stood in a realm, calm and gracious, where there were winding rivers running clear and sparkling through fields full of cowslips. These stood tall and with drooping heads, each one fragrant as the very breath of spring when it steals among the fresh green woods. They seemed to smile at me and fall asleep in happiness. ' Dear flowers,' I said, ' I love you one and all ! ' Then

"THEN I FOLLOWED AFTER THEM."

my eyes fell upon fruitful meadows and flowery woods. Elsewhere I beheld all manner of luscious fruits of various colours, shapes and sizes—fairer than any fruits which grow in this cold world. Yet though all was so beautiful to see, believe me when I tell you that the realm was not lit by the light of any sun. Rather was the atmosphere dark, if one may call that sky and air by such a name.

" Around me came people like, yet unlike, those I saw on earth. They were dwarfish in size, but so exquisitely beautiful to behold that I know no words to tell you how lovely they were. Each one had golden hair, and eyes of a merry limpid blue, while their lips were like the rowan-berries when the sun of September lingers in love upon the mountain-side. Their skin was soft and fresh as that of the red trout which lies in the swift stream. But, for all their smallness of stature, never have I seen such beings for courage. Fleet-footed were they as the lightning which leaps from mountain-top to mountain-top. They rode fiery steeds which were not much larger than hares. I found that their food was very simple, and consisted mostly of apples of all kinds, with milk and roots, soft and sweet to the taste.

" Then there was another thing I am fain to remember. From one end of their land to the other no noise of any kind was heard. Sweet silence lay sleeping everywhere, and none sought to disturb her gentle slumber ; speech itself was silent, nor did there ever fall, even perchance, a curse or oath. Within their territory they would not suffer untruthfulness, or treachery. So I dwelt among them with great respect and admiration. Tender friends were they to me, and I grew to love them. Yes, indeed, and one fair maiden I loved as a man loves the first blush of the morning sky when summer is at its height. Ceinwen was her name ; and she dwelt with her people beside a lonely lake, silvery and broad.

" None was so gentle as Ceinwen, and of all those fair people none so goodly to behold. Her hair was golden like that of her companions, but so long and silken that it fell about her in a golden mist. Her touch was as gentle as the fall of a snowflake on the young grass, and her teeth were white as pearls, and as lustrous. She wore a loose, green tunic which fell almost to her slender ankles, leaving uncovered her snowy neck and shoulders.

" When *hiraeth* first snatched at my heart, I told Ceinwen and she put her soft, white arms around my neck, and then, laying her tender cheek by mine, whispered that love was sacred and that the love of parents was a gift like the sun in winter. ' Go, Elfod,' quoth she, ' but come again soon to the land of Hud-a-Lledrith ! ' For the inhabitants of that land come and go as they list, yet in my mind there arose the thought of the evil of my native land and it troubled me greatly. I longed to tell my kith and kin of the beauty and holiness that dwelt in silence, in a silent and sinless world. Oh ! the richness of that world ! Gold and silver are there in such abundance that the children's toys are made of those precious metals, and the land flashes forth their gladsome light from among its fair flowers, while rivers run glittering over gold and silver beds.

" So I came away, yea, friends, I came away. When the time of my departure arrived, they showered precious gifts upon me, and begged me to come again. With my hand on my heart and with tears in my eyes I gave the promise. Promise ! What need was there for that, when among these loving folk dwelt my Ceinwen ? And was I not, after my long sojourn, one of them already ? It was but the desire to look again upon my parents' faces, to touch their dear hands once more, which lured me away. I said that I should long every hour to come again to my beloved land of Hud-a-Lledrith.

" I gathered together the presents which they showered upon me, and for the last time Ceinwen and I wandered hand in hand along the shore of the peaceful lake. How well I remember the light that streamed from her faithful eyes, and the smile that parted her tender lips, as we spake of our joyful reunion and the marriage that was yet to be ! We kissed, and, with her hand in mine, she murmured once again, ' Come again soon,

Elfod ; for Ceinwen will await thee, if need be for ever ! ' Then she turned from me, and I saw tear drops fall like April showers lit by sunbeams.

" They gave me a silver wand and bade me keep it pure and fair ; after which they sped me on my way. So I came again to the land of my birth, while everybody spoke of Elfod, seeking to learn where I had sojourned. Yet, although I spoke much of the goodness and glory of the fair land, I breathed not one word which would let people know its entrance, or its whereabouts. But I told my mother of the riches, the masses of silver and gold, the rocks of that sweet and silent land, and she pressed me sore till I promised to come again, bringing her treasure that would be beyond the dream of avarice.

" I set out with that foolish promise on my lips, and passed through the wood of oak, and ash, and thorn to find the portal of my paradise. Ha ! the woe of it—the smart of it ! With the vision of Ceinwen before me beckoning me sweetly, yet could I not find the path that should lead me to her. Seek as I might, the land of Hud-a-Lledrith lay I knew not where, and with a heart cold, and heavy as a stone, I came back to my native village.

" My mother met me, and tears fell from her sad eyes. ' Elfod,' she said, ' scarcely had you gone, after you had promised to bring me wealth, when two little men leading white mules came to our abode, and asked for you. They said that you had lost your white wand, and that

" A VISION OF ELFOD."

without it you could NEVER hope to enter the secret place ! '

" Then, friends, I knew that for me there

remained upon earth only a life devoted to holy things ; so I entered the monastery, and was anointed with the sacred oil. Yet, in the midst of this life never have I ceased to dwell upon the goodness of that other life, the wealth of love which I once vainly cast away, thus rejecting the perfection of the Tylwyth Têg. O my Ceinwen, my dear ones, when shall I see your fair smiles in the silent land ? "

So he finished speaking. And they left him as he sat, with his head bowed low upon his hands, and the story passed in loving words from lip to lip.

One night, very soon after, when the white moon rode full and clear over the mountain-top, people heard the sound of silver bells wafted up the valley. Some went to their doors, and they told, thereafter, how they saw faintly, and in a mist, a vision of Elfod, radiant and youthful, hand in hand with an angel, whose golden hair lay like the dusky light of sunset around her lovely form. She was pointing upwards to the sky, and, as they passed along amid the sound of the silvery tones, it seemed as though the wind sighed out :

" Yea, Elfod, it has been long, but now you have once more regained the silver wand, Beloved, and there shall be no more night in the land of Hud-a-Lledrith."

Here endeth the story of Elfod the Priest.

VIII

THE WYVERN

THE people of Coed-y-Moch [1] were always in fear. Never for a single moment, night or day, could they shake off the alarm which hung about them like a cloud. And the cause of this will be clear as our story proceeds. At night they cowered in their houses with their hands pressed to their ears to shut out the heartrending screams which seemed to cut the darkness like a jagged knife, or as though horned devils raged at will about the rugged mountains towering up on all sides of the valley. When day poured its cheering light upon the world there was no respite from this terrible panic. For, even in broad daylight, the loathsome winged snake came and went at its will ; yea, and worse than all besides, lay in evil ambush for any who might, perchance, approach its gruesome haunt. Then with a sudden, cruel movement, it would seize in silence upon its victim, crush life from the writhing limbs, and bear away the inanimate form for food. The whole neighbourhood lay under this baleful

[1] Koîd ĕ mōch, wood of the pigs

92

influence, and like weary captives looked longingly
for a daybreak which should bring deliverance.

Sometimes the monster lay and sunned itself
upon the pebbly shores of Cynwch[1] Lake, and
there, with its slimy folds all uncoiled, would lie
and gaze with lacklustre look across the dancing
waves. At times one could see it creeping, with
hateful, stealthy movements, here and there upon
the fertile slopes of Moel Othrum,[2] jerking its
cumbersome form into uncanny humps as it made
its way in quest of food, and leaving a slimy track
behind it. To this day such venom remains as
visible poison on the mountain-slopes, and whoever
comes thither avoids placing his feet upon such
an evil spot.

The hunger of the loathly creature passed the
comprehension of man : with a huge, gaping
mouth, and cavernous belly, the Wyvern seemed
to have no limit to its powers of digestion, and its
wings would beat with lazy enjoyment as it lay and
chewed the red food of its choice. Sometimes in
its greed it would swallow a lamb at a gulp. When
it killed a beast it bore the carcase to a tree,
fastened itself by winding its tail about the
branches, then, placing the victim between its
body and the trunk of the tree, twined its eager
length, round and round, closer and closer, till the
animal was a pulp and its bones crushed to pieces.
Then, with slow motion of its slavering jaws,

---

[1] Kinūch.   [2] Moil Othrūm, the bare hill of Othrum.

the Wyvern, spreading its warm, slimy body over the soil, sucked the goodness from its raw food. Yet it did not always choose flesh, but stole the fruit of the trees, and with its long and whitish tongue stripped the orchards almost bare.

It flew at night, and, as it flew, screamed with soul-stirring anguish so that men shuddered to hear the sound. Its wings, which were not large for its bulk of body, beat the air with a dull flap, softly and somewhat noiselessly, like the flight of an owl. Its glowing, greenish eyes had keen and penetrating sight, for often, when flying high in mid-air, the Wyvern would swoop suddenly upon some unprotected fold, or traveller wandering in the darkness, and a startled scream, only too quickly smothered, would tell of another victim.

In vain men offered great rewards for its destruction. One cunning old fellow, the wizard who lived in Ganllwyd,[1] strove earnestly to put an end to these terrible sufferings. For many nights and days he pondered, and tried to devise means to slay the Wyvern, and he was thought by the people of those parts to be a man of great cleverness. When the Lord of Nannau cried that he would give three-score head of cattle to him who slew the evil creature, and others came forward and named valuable gifts which they would add as a reward for the terrible feat, this clever old man strove more eagerly to win the wealth. But

[1] Ganllūid

all his efforts were unavailing. The woeful wailing still pierced the night, and by day the distant yet visible form of the Wyvern spread menace from the mountain-side. Then, also, to make matters worse, the Wyvern was growing older and more wary, and to entrap it, or slay it, became daily a task of greater difficulty. To hear its great body hurtle through the darkness, dealing woe and evil as it sped, was awful, and frequently at the sound men fell swooning to the earth. Yet what could be done ?

The Wyvern could attract animals by a kind of spell. If it looked into the eyes of a beast, that creature was doomed. Like the moth which circles around a candle till in the end its charred body falls a voluntary offering into the flame, so every creature that gazed upon the livid green eyes of this winged snake was seized, and held by an awful fascination. With an indescribable meekness such a victim went, step by step, nearer to the watching, luminous eyes, till at last, intoxicated by some unknown power, it passed insensibly, one may suppose, into the soft, slimy folds of the expectant Wyvern.

Yet the cunning Llwyd [1] of Ganllwyd prepared a plan whereby he might slay it, or, if the powers so ordered, catch the vicious monster. He made a bold bid for its blood, and in this wise. Wales had long been famous for its archers. Other

[1] Llūid, grey.

nations copied the skill of the bowman's craft from the swift Welsh, and carried the knowledge to other lands to win great battles against their foes. So old Llwyd hired a dozen of the keenest archers, men whose arrows sped from the bow as a lightning flash speeds from the dark clouds upon the trembling earth, and he placed them on many a crafty coign of vantage. Yet it was never possible to catch even a glimpse of the Wyvern on the days when the bowmen were waiting. It was as though some subtle knowledge came to its brain, and bade it beware. So the plan of Llwyd came to naught, and the Wyvern still screamed through the darkness of the night. But Llwyd continued to frame cunning schemes, and the threescore cows were so rich an offer that every man of enterprise in that district desired to slay or capture the winged snake.

Now there lived among the shepherds of Cwm Blaen y Glyn [1] a youth whose mind leaped towards the prize as a little child springs joyfully to meet its father. He was not yet twenty-one years old, and was strong and sturdy beyond the average of the race of man. From childhood his strength had risen and swelled with him as the life-giving sap toughens the limbs of the oak-tree, and Meredydd was known far and wide for his prowess. By the strength of his hands alone he tore open the gaping mouths of wolves, or wrenched the

[1] Kūm Bline ĕ Glin, the valley of the end of the glen.

deep-seated bough from the parent tree. At wrestling none was his equal, for, when the spirit was strong in his heart, he had the strength of many men, and held his adversary like a little child in his grasp.

Yet Meredydd was gentle withal, and used his strength only for righteous purposes ; and the thought of the Wyvern, and the evil which it wrought, burned in his brain red-hot, giving him no rest by day or night. When he heard the thrilling screams pass overhead Meredydd [1] ground his white teeth with anger, and tossed his black hair with the defiance of the royal beast brought to bay

So at this time he came down from the mountain, nor said one word to man of his intention, for he desired that the purpose of his heart should not be known till the deed was accomplished, and his race rejoiced in deliverance. For Meredydd feared failure. Yes, truly, he feared it as some craven returned home early from the wars might fear the mocking laugh of man, or, still worse, the shrill reproach of woman, as he passed to and fro along the streets of his village home. Yet he told the secret to one fair being, although he spoke not a word to man, and, when he spoke of his intention, so modest was. he that the blush came to his swarthy cheek as the rich hues of sunset are oft-times flung with strange suddenness across the

[1] Meréddith.

8

western sky. When Ellyw [1] saw that sign she knew that purpose was indeed strong in Meredydd's heart, and that she need say nought to encourage or dissuade him. Thus she was wise, although she loved him with all the tenderness of the springtide of life.

Ellyw, therefore, bent low her fair face till the golden hair hid the smile of pride which rippled around her lips, and said simply :

" Go, Meredydd, and my thought and my heart will keep constant company with your absence. Yet remember the words of the cunning man of Ganllwyd, when he said that whoever would slay the Wyvern must wear a dress of steel. Yea, and he added that whoever approached the monster without such a garb would speedily pass into the realms of silence where sun and stars are for ever hidden."

" True," answered Meredydd, " and full well I know the words, and the man ; and I have thought long and anxiously about them, as I sat and kept the browsing sheep upon the mountain-side. There are men, Ellyw, whose words leap from their mouths as living things endowed with life beyond man's comprehension. Llwyd spake thus, and knew not what he said. Nor did I know the meaning of the utterances, till, having cried aloud amidst the silence of the wise, old hills, their wisdom spoke in response to man's eager

[1] Élliu.

questioning and taught me how to act. I shall go with a dress of steel, but not such a dress as Llwyd described."

So they parted. Meredydd passed out from the haunts of men, having for company his two faithful hounds and the glorious resolution of his heart ; while Ellyw, the daughter of Hafodfraith,[1] returned to sojourn with her kinsfolk.

The world is full of courage and heroism. We see this day by day. Even the creatures of the lower ranks of life show us their bravery. Yet whoever went so bravely to so direful a deed as this simple shepherd lad of Cwm Blaen y Glyn ? The words of the wizard and the thought of the foe each strove to make his path heavy ; while the bright, blue eyes of Ellyw shone before him like two guardian angels beckoning him onward. Then, too, he thought of the threescore cows, and in his mind he heard their lowing as they came home at nightfall to be milked ; and, as he remembered the little white farm which stood vacant on the mountain yonder, he peopled it with many a pleasant thought as he strode onward. Yet was he wary and wise, nor frail in his purpose.

By the side of the pathway he had chosen stood the Monastery of the Standard, whose inmates knew Meredydd and loved his merry face and valiant form. He turned in at the gates, passed up to the entrance, and blew loudly upon the horn

[1] Havod vrayth, summer dwelling streaked.

to tell of his arrival. Then the kindly old priests of the monastery thronged hastily around him, asking for news, and pressing him to take refreshment. So he sat, and talked, and fed upon the food they placed before him ; yet, when he rose to depart, he said :

" Friends, for ye are indeed friends to me, trust me and help me in my hour of need. Ye are kindly and know the thoughts which assail the heart of youth. I go on a quest, and need your prayers. So pray for me, but lend me also the glittering axe which fell from heaven, and rests beneath your altar."

Then the eldest and most saintly of the priests looked on Meredydd and read as on an open page the secret of his resolve. He spake no word, but rose and fetched the axe carved with mystic words and said by men to have fallen from heaven. For, long since, it was found one morning quivering in the oaken door of the monastery, and none knew whence it came. He placed the weapon in the shepherd's hands, and, looking long and lovingly into Meredydd's eyes, said :

" Go ! in God's name, go ! and our prayers shall rise urgently to the throne of heaven. For you go upon the errand of mercy."

Then Meredydd was fain at heart, nor was it long before he lit upon the trail of the Wyvern— a trail which lay like a band of death along the hill-side. It was near Cynwch Lake he saw the trail, and he followed it cunningly and withal speedily, up the hill-slopes, through the young

" HE PLACED THE WEAPON IN THE SHEPHERD'S HANDS."

woods merry with the greenery of spring and bright with the dancing of the daffodils, till across the wood he came to the open pastures beyond. There, with its slithering coils all limp in sleep, with its length all along a milk-white hawthorn hedge, lay the hateful Wyvern. Thus the creature rested peacefully amid the blossoms of May, as sometimes an evil thought will lie hidden among the pure resolves of youth, and none can tell that it is there.

So vile was its appearance that the heart of Meredydd stopped beating at the sight ; and he loathed his task ! Then there arose the memories of the cruel past ; and the thought of the gentle Ellyw, and the kindly priests, ran through his brain like crystal, life-giving drops of healing ; and he stole cautiously towards the monster's horrid head.

Now as Meredydd had passed away from the monastery he knew not that the cunning eye of Llwyd watched him from the old hut opposite the wood. Yet so it was, and reading resolution in the young shepherd's bearing, Llwyd had tracked Meredydd from afar, and now waited the issue of his venture ; for he, too, as we have heard, coveted the kine and the rich rewards which should fall to the slayer of the Wyvern.

But Meredydd, thinking only of his lofty purpose and the patience of Ellyw when once she dug him from the pit into which he had fallen while searching for a lost sheep on the mountain, went all the more heedfully towards the foe. He felt,

with skilful thumb, the keen edge of the axe,
and knew that it would not fail him. Again he
thought of the loving, tireless patience of Ellyw,

" SHE DUG HIM FROM THE PIT."

the maid, as she toiled to save his life. Once more
he heard the sob of her dear breath as she cleared a
path to rescue him, and, at the thought, his spirit
rose like flame before the wind, and leaped and

licked around his heart. Then the knowledge sped into his brain that the whitethorn was one mass of bloom, and that nothing on the wide earth could make the Wyvern so drunken with rich, swooning sleep as the heavy odour of that fragrant flower. So his plans grew clearer in his mind, the cold sweat of fear dried upon him, and he felt that his was the victory.

He crept along the near side of the hedge till he found an opening near the Wyvern's head ; yet, even as he peeped through the gap, one baleful, green eye unclosed its lazy lid and looked venomously upon him. But sleep closed up the monster's brain as the darkness of night falls upon and hides the marshy swamp, and Meredydd crept out to deal the fatal blow.

As he passed the nostrils of the Wyvern, its breath came forth as the pestilence which travels by night, and Meredydd well-nigh sank before its hateful stench and the heat of its passage. But he recovered, rose to his full height, and, with the muscles of his arms straining like steel rods under the grip of his hands upon the haft of the axe, he struck a blow that sent the echo throbbing over the hill-side, and the head of the Wyvern fell asunder at his feet. But his peril was great, for the death agonies of that enormous body were not easy to avoid, and Meredydd could not leap aside before the writhing tail caught him with cruel force and stretched him low upon the grass of the meadow.

"HE CREPT ALONG THE . . . HEDGE."

Then, as he lay motionless and white as death, the crouching figure of Llwyd crept upon the scene. With rapid eye he took in the details, and mad jealousy seized him. Since he had failed to slay the Wyvern he resolved that misery should dog the steps of the youth whose courage and simple faith had fairly surpassed his own skill and witchcraft. But, as he stepped forth to do a vile deed, he saw that Meredydd opened his eyes, and raised himself upon his elbow, so he withdrew to the shelter of the wood, shaking with rage, and casting in his mind how to bring evil upon the shepherd lad.

Meredydd slowly raised himself. He felt cold and hot by starts, then a chill as of death swept over him, and he knew not whether he lived or was dead ; but his heart revived as he looked upon the Wyvern and recollected the deed which gave him the rewards, and Ellyw. As his strength and courage came to him, he rose to his feet, and, cutting out the monster's tongue as a token of victory, he bore this and the axe to the good priests of the Monastery of the Standard. They gave him wine, and, bidding him rest, made haste to carry the good news far and wide to the people of Coed-y-Moch. Ere nightfall hundreds of rejoicing eyes gazed greedily upon the hated form of the Wyvern, and the glad folk praised the shepherd youth who had delivered them from the thrall and shame. Men wondered at the power

"DRAGGED THE HUGE WINGED SNAKE."

of the blow which had cloven that enormous skull; they measured out the Wyvern's length and marvelled at the sharp-pointed wings now drooping in the black, oozy blood which fell in heavy gouts from the wound and flowed slowly down the slope of the hill. On the morrow they dug a mighty grave, and with great difficulty dragged the huge winged snake to its depths. Above the grave they built a cairn to mark the spot where Meredydd won his victory, and ever since that day the hill has been called the Hill of the Wyvern. Men call the cairn " The Wyvern's Grave," and every year when spring returns, youths and maidens go forth to garland the stones with sweet-scented sprays of whitethorn.

But at the Monastery of the Standard Meredydd lay at death's door. Many a visitor called to see the deliverer, the saviour of the people of Coed-y-Moch; but the priests with anxious look told how the poison of the winged snake had entered the blood of the shepherd lad so that he lay all unconscious of the world, and spoke words which had no meaning.

Then came among others the cunning Llwyd of Ganllwyd, and asked for news. He was met by the worthy old Aneurin,[1] abbot of the monastery, whose eye could read all secrets. And when Llwyd knew how grievously the fever held Meredydd a baleful gleam of triumph shone from

---

[1] Ánḗirin.

his eyes. Yet he was not aware that he had shown his delight at the dire woe of the young shepherd. But the old abbot saw it and knew the dangers which beset Meredydd's path. Still, he gave a courteous welcome to the wizard, and praised him for his attempts to slay the Wyvern. Yea, and he placed before him good meat and comforting drink, so that Llwyd departed well satisfied from the monastery.

But as he paced down the path to the entrance gates the abbot watched him sadly with shaded eyes, then, shaking his head, he murmured, " 'Tis well the lad bides with us ; but are there others whom Llwyd can injure ? Time will show Aye, time will show us everything."

IX

MEREDYDD [1]

THE SEQUEL TO " THE WYVERN "

So the good priests of the Monastery of the Standard watched carefully over Meredydd, and brought him safely through the illness caused by the evil blows and venom of the Wyvern. They knew of medicinal herbs, they insisted on rest, and they fed him with good homely fare till his blood flowed rich and free once more.

Then the word went round that Meredydd was restored, and the people came to bring him his gifts. Aye, and the Lord of Nannau [2] came himself, and placed the three score of cattle under the charge of the priests against the time when the shepherd youth should come and take them home. So many gifts there were that Meredydd knew that from henceforth he was no longer a poor shepherd, but could take his place among the great people of the district, and he resolved that his conduct for the future should make it possible for him to add to his wealth.

---

[1] Meréddith (accent on the second syllable).   [2] Nannãi.

Amid the feasting and revelry which followed the death of the hateful winged snake, Meredydd's heart was loyal to the past, and directly he grew strong enough to move his limbs freely, he longed the more to go to show himself to Ellyw. What was she thinking about his deed ? Did she wonder at his absence ? Why had no message come from Hafodfraith to assure him that all was well ? But now all folk had given him of their goodwill, and he was free to go from the monastery. Yet, before he went, Aneurin, the old priest, led him aside and whispered words of caution. He told him that he was not free to speak very clearly, but he knew enough to bid him be on his guard against treachery. So Meredydd went forth to seek Ellyw.

He passed blithely over the road he had traversed to encounter the Wyvern. Then the future was unknown, and his intentions were buried in his heart ; but now his name was on everybody's lips, and wealth had poured in by reason of his bravery. Just as before, the vision of Ellyw shone clearly in his mind, and he longed earnestly to see her once more. One word of praise from her was worth all the world beside ; and his footsteps became more rapid as he approached the haunts so familiar to him.

As he drew near to Ellyw's house he could almost hear his heart beat, so deep was his emotion ; but her parents met him before he

"HER PARENTS MET HIM."

reached the door, and told him that the maiden was from home.

" And why have you not been here before this Meredydd ? " said her mother.

Meredydd looked at her in astonishment.

" I could not come," he replied, " for I have been ill, and the priests of the Monastery of the Standard have been restoring me to life."

The parents exchanged glances, they began to realize that the stories which had been brought to their ears were false, but they did not know of the hatred of Llwyd of Ganllwyd. While gladness abounded among men, anger and bitter resentment ruled the life of Llwyd because the young shepherd lad had carried off the rewards which he himself had striven to obtain. Yet the good old abbot of the monastery read the mischief, and knew full well that the wizard would strive to take revenge for his imaginary wrongs.

The three people, so dear to one another, and each so anxious for the absent Ellyw, stood and talked long and earnestly about the events which had occurred, and, as they spoke, the matter grew clearer. Someone must have spread a wrong report. It had been told at Hafodfraith that Meredydd had gone to spend his time in feasting and dancing among the people at Coed-y-Moch, and had forgotten his home and former friends. In bitter sorrow Ellyw had gone away to spend her lonely days at her sister's home, far

9

away beyond the mountain; and Meredydd, with her parents' advice, departed at once to seek her and show her the evil that had been accomplished.

So he went, but at the house of Ellyw's sister he was once more disappointed. Ellyw had set out for her home and should have arrived there by that time. Meredydd turned away, sad at heart, and without waiting a moment bent his steps homeward.

A thick white mist had fallen like the skirts of a giant's robe over the heads of the mountains, and rolled ever lower as the night advanced. A strange foreboding tore at Meredydd's heart, making the way weary and long; but, had he known all, his anxiety would have been increased tenfold. Ellyw had not arrived home, for, by the arts of Llwyd, she had wandered far and wide from her proper path. All through the day she had striven to retrace her steps, but the difficulties increased as her strength grew less; and, after many weary, lonely hours, she sank down sadly upon a flat rock, and sobbed bitterly.

As she sat thus Llwyd appeared, and, with an evil leer, told her that Meredydd was unfaithful to her, that he was at Coed-y-Moch, feasting and merry-making with the people, and made much of by the maidens.

"Aye, and it is said," quoth Llwyd, "that his heart has gone out to one, the fair daughter of the

Lord of Nannau, and that the wedding will soon take place." Then he disappeared, and left the lonely Ellyw still more solitary by reason of his words.

As she sat sorrow-stricken a mountain bird flew down to a crag near by and uttered a frightened, plaintive cry. " Poor bird," she said, " what anguish stirs your heart ? " She rose, and followed the bird as it flew away. Once more it settled, and gave its sorrowful cry, so she strove to approach it. Again the bird flew ahead, and thus she followed till the mist enwrapped her, and amid pathless ways she heard naught save the cry of the bird. Suddenly her foot sank into a soft yielding spot, and lo ! she was in a morass. With all her efforts, exhausted as she already was, Ellyw was unable to get clear. Alone on the bleak mountain, gripped by the deadly morass, led thither by the arts of the cruel Llwyd, the poor girl seemed doomed to a sad and early death.

She began earnestly to repeat " Our Father," and the words brought her comfort. She thought of Meredydd and Hafodfraith. The sunny days of the past rose to her mind, and she dwelt with gladness on the comradeship she had enjoyed with Meredydd. Why had he so easily forgotten her ? She thought of her old parents ; and, as this memory came to her, she burst into tears when she considered how lonely they would be without her.

" Oh ! Meredydd, Meredydd ! " she wailed, " why did you go away ? "

As she spoke it seemed to her that a distant noise broke the dumb silence which lay around. Was it only her imagination ? Or was there actually some sound ? The air grew rapidly colder ; she listened in vain ; but she had now sunk to her knees in the morass. She prepared herself to die. Yet, once again, she strove to cry aloud. " Would that Meredydd knew where I was ! Meredydd, Meredydd ! "

Then, indeed, there came an answering cry from someone shouting with all his might, " Ellyw ! Ellyw ! " What could it mean ? With all her remaining strength she replied, " Here ! Here ! Come quickly ! " Then her head fell on her breast. Ellyw had swooned.

In a few minutes Meredydd came to the edge of the morass, and saw the sad plight of the girl. As he had pursued his sad way homeward, he determined to win Ellyw come what might. He would go and tell her of his victory over the Wyvern, and explain how it was won for her alone. She should see his rewards, the threescore of cattle and all the other gifts ; and with these thoughts in his mind he had hurried on. In his haste he had missed his way, and soon found himself wandering on the wild wastes of the mountains. Yet in his loneliness he had cried " Ellyw ! Ellyw ! " Then through the sombre stillness that enwrapped him,

THE WYVERN

"Ere nightfall hundreds of rejoicing eyes gazed greedily upon the hated form of the wyvern."

(Plate 5)

THE STRAND OF THE BITTER CRY

"Father ! I went erewhile to the cellars, and lo ! they are half full of water, and in that water strange fish move heavily to and fro."   *(Plate 6)*

as if in answer to his wild cry, he thought he had heard the distant voice of the one whom he loved so dearly. He paused, and listened, with his heart beating wildly. How could it be Ellyw in this wild and lonely place ? Again he heard the faint cry, and recognized the agony in the voice. He sprang forward, searching wildly until he found the unconscious girl. He leaned over, and with the utmost gentleness, and using every care, he dragged her from the place which she had thought would be her grave.

Although she was half dead, yet she was life itself to Meredydd. Even as the sun in spring brings back life to the chilled and sleeping trees, so the very sight of Ellyw inspired him with the resolution to bring her safely home. He chafed her cold hands, wrapped her warmly in his shepherd's plaid, and, holding her like a child in his strong young arms, he passed heedfully down the mountain-slope. Ere long he saw the eyelids open, and the sad, blue eyes looked wonderingly upward. He bade her be still, and soon she sank into a soft restoring sleep. A shepherd's hut, upon which Meredydd chanced, gave them timely shelter, and when the day broke the mist had rolled away. They could see the distant pathway leading like a long, grey silken thread over the mountains to the home at Hafodfraith.

Before they reached the home of Ellyw all had been explained, and they knew the cunning arts

"WRAPPED HER . . . IN HIS SHEPHERD'S PLAID."

that had separated them. Then Meredydd recalled the earnest words of Aneurin, the priest, and understood the jealousy which rankled in the heart of Llwyd. He was anxious for the future, yet, as it chanced, even that load was lifted from his heart, for, soon after, some shepherds found Llwyd lying dead at the foot of a precipice. The

" THE GOOD PRIESTS . . . BROUGHT ALL THE GIFTS."

thick mist which had brought Meredydd and Ellyw together had separated the cruel wizard from the light of day ; and he passed with all his skill and hatred into the abodes of the dead.

Great was the joy at Hafodfraith when the young shepherd led Ellyw home in safety. Yet a short time after, this happiness was increased by the marriage of Meredydd and Ellyw, and the whole neighbourhood came together to celebrate their union.   Meredydd was loved for his courage and gentleness, his faithfulness and his simple heart ; Ellyw was dear to everyone for her beauty, and goodness and patience.   They went to live in the white farm on the mountain-slope, and thither the good priests of the Monastery of the Standard brought all the gifts bestowed upon Meredydd for his victory over the Wyvern.

As time went on Meredydd's happiness was increased and his wealth multiplied.   His children were bold and resolute.   They loved and deeply respected their parents, for they often heard from those who knew the story how their father and mother had come together.   So great a deed as the victory over the Wyvern sank deep into their hearts ; and thus it has come to pass that the descendants of Meredydd and Ellyw have that well-known coat of arms which depicts a Wyvern, an axe, and a shepherd's crook upon an azure field.

"THEY OFTEN HEARD . . . THE STORY."

X

THE STRAND OF THE BITTER CRY

THE waves of war have often swept over the rugged land of Wales and dyed its green valleys with the red blood of death. The brave children of the land of the west have struggled against the invader on many a battlefield, and the eternal hills have looked down on many a brave deed, and hearkened unto many a sigh as the spirit has fled from its earthly companion. Like other lands, Wales has seen her children make war one upon another ; for greed turns the heart of man from gentleness and leads into strange paths those who yield to its evil influence. In the olden times of which we hear so much and yet know so little, the sight of a few sheep might impel men to slaughter their fellows, and leave their wives in widowhood, and their children sorrowing orphans.

> The mountain sheep are sweeter,
>   But the valley sheep are fatter ;
> We therefore deemed it meeter
>   To carry off the latter.

We made an expedition,
  We met an host and quelled it ;
We forced a strong position,
  And killed the men who held it.

We there, in strife bewildering,
  Spilt blood enough to swim in,
We orphaned many children
  And widowed many women.
The eagles and the ravens
  We glutted with our foemen,
The heroes and the cravens,
  The spearmen and the bowmen.

We brought away from battle,
  And much their land bemoaned them,
Two thousand head of cattle,
  And the head of him who owned them.
Ednyfed, King of Dyfed,
  His head was borne before us ;
His wine and beasts supplied our feasts,
  And his overthrow our chorus.

So sings a poet about those olden days ; and thus it was, perhaps, that, at the end of the year after the slaughter of Elidir Mwynfawr,[1] there came men to Ystrad Clwyd,[2] in the north of Caernarvon, to avenge the blood of their king. Full of anger did they come, with fierce hearts beating to slay, and pillage, and take toll for the deed of blood. In their swift onslaught they fell upon Caernarvon, and burnt it to ashes. Then

[1] Elídir mūinvaur. Elidir greatly kind.
[2] Estrad Klūid, Vale of the gate.

they trampled with heavy foot upon the ruins, laughing loud and long at the scene of desolation which their eyes beheld.

Yet when Rhun, the son of Maelgwyn Gwynedd,[1] came and saw their handiwork his heart sank with sorrow ; yea, it sank heavily, as a stone sinks through the water. For in that town had lived one whom he loved, and whose eyes were now closed for ever in the fast sleep of death. But Rhun felt more than sorrow. Grief, forsooth, was the first-comer to his heart ; then after grief came passion, red-hot, pulsing passion—pulsing like lead as it runs through the furnace to the mould beneath. In this anger he turned, and called, " Who will follow me to beat down the bitter foe who hath done this deed ? " Then answered many a warrior, deep-voiced and stern, " I will follow thee ! " And when Rhun started on the march a mighty host went with him, and at their head strode the son of Indo Hên[2], the chief of men.

They went with subtilty, and swiftness, and came upon the foe on the shores of the River Gweryd [3] in the north. Then, with such suddenness as one sees when some huge rock breaks loose from its ancient bed, and speeds, thundering and crushing all before it, on its powerful rush to the

[1] Rheen. Mailgwin Gwineth, iron white of Gwynedd.
[2] Indo Hane, Indo the old.
[3] Gwerid.

"THE MEN OF CAERNARVON SWEPT THEIR FOES BEFORE THEM."

valley, so one army fell upon the other.   Amid the clash of steel, the clatter of blade upon buckler, the shivering of pikes, the singing of javelins, the rattling of hauberk, and the ringing of helmets, the stern shout arose, " Remember Caernarvon." Whereupon the men of Caernarvon swept their foes before them as the autumn blast picks up, whirls, and scatters the fallen leaves ; so that when the silver moon stole out from the bosom of the hills, the men who had gone to Ystrad Clwyd lay stiff and stark under her pitying light.

On the morrow, the men of Caernarvon took their pick from the inhabitants of the land. Widows and orphans stood helpless before them ; and not only they, but men of high degree, princes, people whose privilege it was to wear the golden torque of royalty.   From all these the conquerors chose whom they would, and led them back as slaves and servants to the realms of the north. Such wealth and plunder they had never possessed before ; and this was the fruit of their victory.

Now among these slaves of lofty lineage there was a young Saxon, the wearer of a golden torque. Highborn he was, and accustomed to rule rather than serve.   Yet such was his wisdom, and such his natural gentleness and courtesy, that, ere long, all with whom he came in contact sang the praises of Edred, the Saxon slave.   Rhun himself would often go and converse with him, and ask him about the story of his youth, about his kith and kin.

As time went on Edred was appointed to be a personal attendant of Rhun, and daily found fresh favour. But Rhun would often take notice that, when Edred was alone, his eyes looked far away as though they saw something beyond the lofty mountain peaks, and, from time to time, a deep sigh would escape his lips like a worn-out captive stealing from a sad prison. Then Rhun, as he grew to love him better, and more fully understood that far-away look and heavy sigh, came one day, unexpectedly, and, laying his hand on the young Saxon's shoulder, said :

" Tell me, Edred, why your heart is heavy ? Are we not kind to you ? "

Then Edred made answer, and said :

" Kind indeed you are, and more than kind. Somehow you, who once were enemies, are, as it were, brothers to me. Yet, when I think of those who reared me and nurtured me in my childhood, sadness steals over me as the greyness steals over the land at eventide. This, O Rhun, you can understand full well, for the Welsh love their kinsfolk dearly, and are true to them."

Then Rhun stood silent with his head bowed in thought. In silence, also, he turned away and a tear stole from his brave, blue eyes. He strode to his home, and all that day Edred did not see him again. But at night a messenger visited the young Saxon, and he carried with him rich presents of gold and silver, and jewelled garments. He said that Rhun had set Edred free, but he would fain see him again, if, perchance, he ever cared to come and sojourn with the Welsh at Caernarvon. Then Edred was both glad and sorrowful. In haste he went to Rhun and told him that from his heart he thanked him. His desire was, indeed, to visit his own people, yet he would return again to his dear friends among the mountains of Wales to show them his gratitude by his devotion. So he made all preparations for his departure.

Now, in the days of Rhun, there lived in those parts a rich and exceedingly lovely lady named Gwendud.[1] She was as proud as she was beautiful, and held her head in fine disdain whenever she passed through the throng of men who stood to watch her beauty. She was but young, and had many brothers and sisters, yet she differed from them in many ways. They, too, after their own fashion were handsome. But it was in the heart that the difference chiefly lay. For while Gwendud's kindred had resolved to go through the land of Wales, preaching the glories and bliss of those who followed the Christ, and striving to win their countrymen from a pagan condition, she had no such desire. So that the brothers and sisters had totally different habits from Gwendud. Her great wish was to remain in that neighbourhood and wed some great and

[1] Gwendid.

noble prince. " Yes," quoth she, with proud look and upturned brow, " my husband shall wear the golden torque. I will not mate with anyone of less degree."

As she spake thus her eyes would sparkle as the blue gems sparkle at the edge of the coronet of some king, and her bosom, white as the soft down of the swan, rose and fell with the resolve of her heart. Truly she was lovely—a vision of the pure spring blossoms flushed with the early crimson of the year, and crowned with the richest gold ; and many there were who loved her, yet feared to tell her of their love. Men even said that much as they admired her beauty, they greatly feared to win her—as one may watch the beauty and the strength of some splendid steed yet dread to ride it.

At that time came Hywel,[1] the son of a wealthy neighbour, and told Gwendud of his love for her. With dark and resolute eyes he looked her through and through, and dared proclaim his love and his desire to win her. As he looked in her eyes she read his resolve, and felt that she would willingly yield to him ; but her heart was set on a golden torque, and the nobility that came therewith. For though Hywel was rich, and would one day be still more wealthy, he was not the possessor of the wreath of twisted gold. So she turned coldly away, stilling her heart and its emotions,

[1] Hewel.

as the rigid ice checks the throbbing surface of the lake when the moon is full.

As she stood silent Hywel said :

" Why do you not answer me, O Gwendud ? "

Then, with a low, cruel laugh, she replied :

" Does Hywel wear the torque ? "

" Why, no," he answered, " I am not royal ! "

She made no reply. But when Hywel urged her to tell him her meaning, in measured distant words, she spoke her resolution. So cold was her speech that it fell like a chill upon the youth, and he went silently, despondently, to his home.

Yet, as Hywel thought long and earnestly about Gwendud, the resolve came to him to win a golden torque by fair means or by foul, for he knew he could not live without her. But he was often in despair, for the wearing of a golden wreath is so high an honour that few attain unto it. However, since the possession of a torque was the sole condition, and this was not altogether impossible, Hywel determined not to rest until he gained one. So he went towards Caer Rhun,[1] near Bangor, to see what the future might bring him.

It befell that Hywel came to Caer Rhun at the time that Edred the Saxon, having obtained permission of Rhun, was about to set forth on his journey to the lowlands beyond the mountains. Men talked of his forthcoming departure, of his favour with Rhun, and of his golden torque. As

[1] Car rheen, Castle of Rhun.

"DOES HYWEL WEAR THE TORQUE?"

Hywel heard these words his eyes grew small and sharp as the hard and glittering diamond, and he drew near to hear yet more.

Quoth one, " Edred goes by way of Conwy, and far beyond, so he needs a guide ; yet who can go in the harvest of the year ? "

" True," said another ; " yet, if no guide be found, Rhun so loves him that he himself will lead him on his way."

Hearing these words Hywel went swiftly to Edred, and, with a face as open as the summer sky, offered to guide the Saxon.

" I have but just arrived at Caer," said Hywel, " but already I have heard men speak of you and tell of your departure, and, as I myself must go towards Conwy, if you so desire, I will gladly show you the safest and quickest way. Since my childhood I have lived here, and none knows the paths better than I."

The Saxon youth gladly accepted the offer of the guide, never thinking of the treachery that lurked in Hywel's heart like some foul monster which, eager for food, sits in a den whose front is adorned with the honeysuckle and tender ivy. For Hywel's intention was to slay Edred, and gain possession of the golden torque.

So they two set out and came right merrily on their journey till the road forked, so that one path ran smooth and level along the low-lying ground, while another climbed the secret places of the

IDWAL OF NANT CLWYD

"The old man looked at them and said." 'Where are my mother and my father and my wife?'

(Plate 7)

EINON AND OLWEN

"They gave him gold and silver, rich jewels without number."

(Plate 8)

mountains. Here Hywel urged that they should take the upper path, for he told how the lower was infested with ravening wolves, and by a race of men more fierce even than those cruel enemies.

" Up on the mountain paths," he said, " the way is narrow, and often difficult, but it is free from such bitter foes, while the path by the plain lies through thick woods where the aggressor can lurk unseen."

Thus he lured Edred away from the beaten track, and the haunts of man, to the wild and unfrequented places of the mountains, in order that he might be more free to do the cruel deed to which his passion impelled him. And Edred, all unsuspecting, went with his guide, listening to his merry conversation.

When they came to the river, which has ever since that time been called Afon-Lladd-Sais,[1] Hywel did the evil that lay in his heart. The place was by a narrow, rushing stream, and all around were great boulders sheltering them from any passer-by who might chance that way. Away below their feet the great slope swept grandly to the wooded plains, and above them the mountains towered superbly to the sky. The sun had set and all was peace and quietness while they stood to watch the glory of the eventide as it lingered tenderly upon the woods and fields of the plain. Then, as they talked, Hywel drew

[1] Avon-llath-sayes, River-kill-Saxon.

back one pace, and, in a flash, drove his knife into Edred's back so that he fell heavily, with one bitter sob, upon the stones on the streamlet's bank, and died.

Hywel stood, looking at the man who a moment before had talked and laughed with him, and now lay so disfigured on the ground. He bent down in haste, and, scarce knowing what he did, he plucked the golden torque from Edred's neck, placed it round his own, then fled in terror from the spot; yea, fled through the fall of the evening, fled through the blackness of the night, nor stayed his fleeting steps until he came with the dawn to the abode of Gwendud. He entered, and said :

" Behold the golden torque ! Give me your hand ! "

But Gwendud, looking upon him, saw that all was not well, and drew back.

" Nay, Hywel," she said, " not yet will I give my hand ; for I must know how you came by the golden circle that gives you princely rank. Full glad am I to see the torque, but I must know more before we can speak of marriage." So she sat down to hearken to what he would say.

Then Hywel let loose the words of his heart till they flowed in tumultuous haste, telling of passionate love, and resolve which knew no restraint. His language poured as some mountain stream, swollen by the winter rains, and held

back painfully by hindering rocks, bursts suddenly
into a free, clear channel, and dashes forward to
the fruitful plain beneath.

When he had finished Gwendud said :

" And did you bury the body ? " This she
said coldly but with deep meaning.

" No ! " said Hywel. " I dared not stop for
that."

" Then you must go forthwith ; nay, say not
one word. Go back with all the speed you may,
and bury Edred deep out of sight. For mark me,
Hywel, should Rhun get to hear of this he will
avenge Edred's blood as surely as the dawn comes
after the darkness of night. Then shall all your
labours be in vain, and marriage for me would
mean widowhood, or worse. Go ! Do not see
me till the deed is accomplished."

So Hywel went with haste, and, coming again
to the place of murder, looked all unwillingly upon
Edred's corpse. Then he commenced to dig a
deep grave in the place that is called to this day
Braich y Bedd.[1] He toiled long and arduously,
and as his task neared completion, he paused to
rest and look awhile over the plain and its broad,
fair woods. As he stood leaning on his mattock,
thinking how strangely quiet was everything in
the world below, from somewhere overhead came
a trembling, rushing sound which grew ever louder,
till, like a peal of thunder, rang out the words :

[1] Brake ĕ Beth, Arm of the grave.

" Woe upon woe ! Vengeance will come ! "

Then, as though the very mountains were awake and answering to the awful sound, the words, " Vegeance will come ! " eddied and bubbled around him, sweeping against his ears and refusing to be shut out. Aye, the very rocks bellowed out against him, " Vengeance will come ! Vengeance will come ! " Three times did this happen, and each time the appalling cry grew louder and more intense, till it seemed to him that the whole earth must hear the accusing sounds, and demand the reason for them. At the third cry Hywel flung down his mattock, and leaping horror-stricken from the spot, went trembling like an aspen-leaf to Gwendud.

As he came before her she said coldly :

" Is the deed done ? "

" No ! " quoth Hywel.

" Why are you in my presence, then, against my wish ? " asked she.

So Hywel explained, and told her of the awful voice that pealed out over the mountain. Whereupon, woman-like, she asked questions, putting before him things of which he had not thought.

" Did you ask when vengeance would come ? "

" Nay," said he, " for I fled heart-stricken from the grave. I would sooner cast the torque into the heart of the deepest mountain lake than reply to that voice of Fear. Yea, Gwendud, I would even put aside all thoughts of marriage rather than answer the unknown accuser ! " So he stood pale and trembling before her, and she looked upon him with eyes as piercing as the lightning-flash. But he went on, " Rather than suffer such terrible

" LEAPING HORROR-STRICKEN FROM THE SPOT."

torture I will go hence to some place of exile and expiate my sin by long years of bitter repentance till time, if it be possible, shall show full atonement for the deed I have committed."

At this Gwendud, seeing his resolve and knowing she stood fair to lose him and his love, yet determined to bend him to her will, spoke softly and with gently impelling words.

" No, Hywel," she said, with love-filled, yearning eyes, eyes which swam like stars before him, " not so. Fear nothing for my sake. But, for our future happiness, go and bury him, and should the cry come again, ask, ' When will vengeance come ? ' Do this, because I love you, and would be yours."

Then, smitten with her gentleness and desiring above all to please her, Hywel, casting fear aside, went again to the spot where the body lay.

He started, once more, his awful task. When the grave was finished he placed therein the stiff form of Edred, and hurriedly set to work to shovel in the earth, to hide the body from his sight. So he continued till the last shovelful was cast and the grave was level with the ground. Then, and not till then, that cry rang out like the trump of doom, " VENGEANCE WILL COME ! " and the echoes sounded, " Vengeance will come ! Vengeance will come ! "

Hywel stood, with his hands before his face, and, in a low quailing voice asked :

" When ? "

And the unseen proclaimer of doom answered :

" In the time of the children, the grand-children, and the great-grandchildren ! "

A deadly silence followed these words, and Hywel stole in fear and trembling from the side of the Saxon's grave.

When he stood again before Gwendud she saw that he had done the deed ; but she waited for his news with all the patience peculiar to women. At last he spoke, and said :

" Gwendud, the voice answered my question ! "

" What did it tell you ? " she asked.

" That vengeance would come in the time of the children, the grandchildren, and the great-grandchildren ! "

Gwendud glanced downwards, and for a time no words passed between them. Then she raised her face, and said quietly, yet with love and admiration in her gaze :

" Hywel, we both shall be dust long before that time arrives ; we need not fear the day ; so I give you my hand and all that is mine."

Her desire was ardently towards marriage ; nay, she insisted on its speedy celebration ; because the judgment for the evil deed was not to fall until the third generation.

Never had there been so splendid a wedding in those parts, nor such a handsome bride. The sun shone brightly in the clear sky ; the guests were resplendent in gay attire of red and purple adorned with sparkling jewels. The bride rode on a white horse caparisoned with splendid harness, and joy flashed from every eye. Since both

Hywel and Gwendud were rich beyond measure, wealth poured in upon them ; for that is the way of this strange world.   When the father of Hywel passed away, they went to live at the castle, which they magnified and adorned with great splendour and luxury, for, by their abode there, it became a palace.   This prince and princess lived such a life as few enjoy.   So abundant was the mirth that never a day passed without music and dancing, and the palace rang with boisterous shouts and giddy pleasure, for Gwendud was a right royal hostess and loved gaiety.

So the years flashed by as some gorgeous cavalcade passes with clatter and laughter through the narrow streets of a town.   Children were born to the joy-loving couple, and, like their parents, turned with pleasure towards the pursuit of enjoyment.   Once in a while the brothers and sisters of Gwendud would come to see their sister ; but she always sighed with relief when they departed.

In course of time the children grew up and married, and, to all appearances, were wedded most happily.   Seven sons there were, and five daughters, fair as the merry flowers of the summer when the sun shines at its greatest height.   As Hywel and Gwendud looked upon their offspring they thought of the voice, and their hearts were soothed as they remembered that vengeance might not fall in their lifetime, nor in that of their children. Then one would say to the other, " Fortunate are we, and blessed beyond ordinary measure in having such children, and in knowing that they may not inherit punishment for our misdeed."

Truth to tell, as the years waxed and waned and dropped into the river of forgetfulness, so the memory of the deed of horror grew fainter, till one would suppose it had in due course almost faded from the parents' minds. Then a grandson was born to Hywel and Gwendud ; the son of their eldest son ; and lo ! another and yet another, till an abundant generation took the place of that which had grown up so merrily. And the old castle and its recent additional buildings still echoed with laughter and the beating feet of the merry dancers. " Aye," quoth Hywel, " better laugh than be sad." After this fashion the years passed swiftly by.

In the ripeness of old age Hywel and Gwendud, hale and hearty as the sturdy oaks of the forest, and beautified with the silvery splendour of the years, stood on a day and watched their descendants. Then came one, and said, " Sire, your friends give you joy. Your grand-daughter Netha has given birth to a son ! " Thus it came to pass that the years had fled, and they two were great-grandparents. They looked at each other ; then Hywel said :

" In the days of the great-grandchildren.

Perhaps not yet, Gwendud, and we may be gone before then."

But so sturdy a line was theirs that it knew no loss by death, and still others were born to swell the numbers. Men marvelled at the family; and people came from far and foreign places to see the number of the generations.

However, it is not given to man to live for ever. A time must come for each of us when the evening shall fall, night steal over the loftiest mountain-peak, and the flashing stars tell silently of heaven. Both Hywel and Gwendud began to feel the chill of eventide; and on a day Gwendud, still harbouring the love of mirth and feasting, said to Hywel:

"Would it not be better to have a banquet for us and our descendants, so that, once again, before we pass hence, we may gather all our sons and daughters, their children and children's children upon our hearth? Let us forget our age in the merry laugh of our descendants!"

Hywel saw that this was good, and word went forth that on the first day of summer a great feast would be given, and all were invited to appear.

Such preparations were made! Hunters were busy tracking the hart royal in the forest, fishermen cast their nets, and not in vain, for a silvery harvest; bakers toiled night and day, making the good, crisp bread and spicy cakes. From the deepest vaults of the palace, cellarers fetched sparkling wines redolent of joy and youth. And anon, all was nearly ready for the festive day.

Meanwhile, Hywel sent to Bangor for skilful players of instruments who should scatter harmony for the dancers, and kindle merry laughter in the hearts of those who listened. Aye, and a Bard was fetched, a man hoary with age, and famed far and wide for his words and the flow of wit and wisdom. Everything was done in the most costly fashion as a prelude to the departure of the aged couple, which must of necessity happen soon after in peace and perfect quietness.

Ah! think you so? Then hearken once again to the voice of prophecy. Doth not winter follow summer? Do not sparks fly upwards? Is not death the sure follower of life, and will not the grave close upon the merry life, that long since lay crowing in the cradle?

When all was ready for the feast, the Bard, bent with years, and pure as winter with his snowy locks and long white beard, turned and spoke to a merry, dark-eyed maid:

" Dost thou know that to-day God will bring vengeance on this place."

" Vengeance, father? " quoth she, " and why? "

" Vengeance, my child," he made answer, " and that for some hoar, some long-forgotten deed done by the old people ere thou wast born, though perchance my own feet had trodden some distance upon this weary pilgrimage."

Then he paused, and the maid looked wonderingly upon the working of the spirit which moved him so strangely. At last he laid an old and trembling hand upon her shoulders and spoke again :

" When thou goest to the cellar in search of mead or wine, look carefully all around, and if thou seest water coming in, and in that water small white fish, come speedily and tell me."

Then he took up his old harp and played low, soul-stirring music so that all marvelled to hear it ; and a dark shadow stole over the faces of Hywel and Gwendud.

Sometime in the midst of the feast, when laughter and wine were flowing freely, the maid came swiftly to the side of the Bard, and with eyes wide open and greatly terrified, she said :

" Father ! I went erewhile to the cellars, and lo ! they are half full of water, and in that water strange white fish move heavily to and fro ! "

" Well, then," he answered, " come now with me, maiden ; come at once, let us flee away for our lives, and indeed, it is high time ! " So they two went swiftly from the hall.

They passed rapidly away from the palace, hearing as they sped the joyous sounds of merry-making and dancing ; but before they left the grounds that surrounded the ancient walls they paused in horror as the sound of the mighty roar of lofty ocean waves leaping against the palace walls broke upon their ears. Then arose a cry, a terrible, heartrending, piercing sound, which sent a cold shiver over their bodies, causing the hair of their heads to stand upright. But they had no time to wait, for already water was sobbing in the grass at their feet, and soon they were running ankle-deep in a frothy foam that hissed around them like the hiss of a thousand vipers. Yet as they went up the hill-side, they left the water ; and, climbing higher and higher, stood at last upon the mountain summit. It was night and very dark. Thus in sorrow and bitter anguish they sat down, waiting for the dawn.

Who can so describe the disclosure of that dawn that he who hears may see what lay before their eyes ? A mighty waste of misty waters ! The boundless sea lay moaning over the land. The old Bard and the young serving-maid alone had escaped from the Palace of Pleasure, and the doom of the years. "Vengeance will come ; vengeance will come !"

Men say (and who can refuse to believe them ?) that, when the wind blows strongly from the east and the tide sinks low, the walls of Hywel's palace are visible to this day. And this is the legend of the Strand of the Bitter Cry.

11

XI

IDWAL OF NANT CLWYD [1]

IN the valley of Nant Clwyd one used to see in the bygone days an old deserted farmhouse. By the side of its prosperous neighbours it looked shabby and forlorn. While plenty and shining contentment seemed to smile about the doors and windows of the other farms, this poor old waif, left bare and desolate in the midst of the fertile valley, seemed to beg for a touch of pity and the glance of compassion. Yet the valley *was* fertile, and the little stream as it purled over its cosy bed seemed to speak of the wealth of the mountains. Why was this picture of desolation painted so clearly on the canvas of nature ? Ah ! that is a story that carries one a long way back, amid strange scenes in another and stranger generation. But come, and we will hear this strange tale of Idwal of Nant Clwyd.

The parents of Idwal were worthy and respectable farming folk, and they lived in the farm at Nant Clwyd. Several children had been

[1] Nant Klūid, brook of the gate.

born to them, but one after the other passed away in childhood. Then, last of all, came Idwal ; and as the rose that blooms late in the spring escapes the cold biting winds which shatter tender petals, so Idwal made his appearance after the sorrows of the family had fled. One need not say he was the light of his parents' eyes. Through him they hoped that their line would be continued. No man dies with an easy mind unless he has someone who, when he is dead, can arrange for his funeral, or who will water his grave with tears, and gladden it with flowers. From whom can one expect such kind offices if not from one's children ? Man loves to believe that there will be a little sorrow after he has departed from this world of time, and what human being is so free from this harmless desire that he can afford to laugh or stare at another ?

One day Idwal went out hunting with a faithful friend. This was Caradog, the son of the people who lived at the farm next to Nant Clwyd. Idwal and Caradog had played together as children, sat side by side at school, and, growing older, had courted, and then married at the same time. For, at the same hour, in the same church, and before the same priest, they had married two sisters. One can imagine how happy these four had been in the green shelter of the dear valleys in the heart of Wales.

Idwal and Caradog started out, and, after a time

at their sport, they came to a dense thicket whose branches so intertwined that they formed a green roof overhead. Here the two friends separated in order that each might track the game more stealthily. Caradog, finding after a while that the day was growing old, and knowing full well that it would take some time to reach their homes, began to make some effort to find Idwal. He called and even shouted ; but in vain. In spite of every effort Idwal remained lost, till at last Caradog departed to tell the news at home. No one slept a wink at Nant Clwyd that night by reason of anxiety, and hopes and fears. Yes, indeed, fears for the worst, and hopes for the best filled every heart.

On the morrow they all went to search for Idwal. The ploughs stood idle in the soil, and the farmyards were strangely quiet. In the wood, however, there was tumult. Men went rapidly searching every nook and corner where Idwal had been lost. But their efforts were in vain. In spite of the warmth of friendship between the two hunters, the tongue of slander began to move busily and shape treachery against Caradog. But his manner was so honest and his face so open, his answers to questions so kindly, that every doubt was killed, causing slander to drink its own blood.

Idwal was sought for with the utmost care. The whole wood was searched, and scarcely a

twig was left untouched. So keen and intent
was the search that one might have thought that

" ALL WENT TO SEARCH FOR IDWAL."

the people in that wood had gone suddenly mad
and wandered in their madness. Their loud

cries lent ears to the wind; but that brought no answer on its wings; not even the smallest cry from Idwal. The testimony of the trembling leaves was the only response that they received to their soul-stirring questions.

After a long, long quest, some of them saw a circle of the Tylwyth Têg near the spot where Idwal had disappeared. Then, truly, all doubt was removed; for they decided at once that Idwal had been unfortunate enough to come under the spell of the small, strange people, and had been lured away by their weird, sweet music to the land of Hud-a-Lledrith.

Gradually all hope of seeing Idwal of Nant Clwyd faded away. His friends said, " We shall see him no more in the land of the living"; and their tears were very bitter as they mourned for his absence. But before he was completely forgotten, a circumstance occurred that brought again his memory in a striking manner. At the end of four months a child was born, who in very truth was just the living image of his father. This child grew to manhood, and filled the place of his father in the hearts of the old grandparents. He also, in due course, was married, and his bride was a young and lovely girl from the neighbourhood. Alas! courtesy and generosity were not among the virtues of her kinsfolk.

Now these two virtues have never been seen apart since the world began. Love-twins are they, yet generosity is the elder of the twain. Each is the life-breath of the other, the other's soul. And say now, those who know, whoever heard of a courteous miser ? Yes, Idwal's son had married into a family of misers who had banished all gentleness, all courtesy, all compassion from their hearts. And woe upon woe, yea, till the heart trembles at the pity of it, greed and the denial of these virtues were the first things they taught their offsprings.

The daughter-in-law was thus. She knew not the warmth which breaks into fire at some kindly deed. Cold in heart was she, cold as the icicle that clings to the mouth of the snow bear's cave.

In the passage of time the father and mother and the wife of Idwal closed their eyes upon this world. Fifty years of joy and sadness, of despair and hope had sped over the heads of the sons of men since Idwal had vanished so secretly. Not one of the sons of man was there so lofty as to avoid the passing of the bitter cup, nor was there one so humble but that he was at times able to spare a drop from the cup of sweetness.

Then came one cold and cheerless day in February ; such a day as sees the trees despair of life, and groan and crack with the chill of winter in their hearts. The children of Nant Clwyd saw through the windows an old, white-haired man, thin and tall, approaching the farm. With trembling steps he drew nearer to the house. In appearance he seemed a beggar ; and, forsooth, he must have been a great stranger to those parts, if he turned his steps to Nant Clwyd in hope of charity ! His clothes lay in miserable rags upon his limbs, and the servants of the spindle-side and their close-eyed mistress, after considering him, mocked him to his face. " Ah ! ah ! " they shrilled in high-pitched, woman's laughter, " the old Irishman ! " And they said

" BADE HIM QUIT THE HOUSE."

to him, " We are not at all surprised to see a man of your condition walk up to the door, and knock thus, without ceremony."

The old man looked at them, and said :

" Where are my mother, and my father, and my wife ? "

The farmer's wife in anger bade him quit the house as fast as he could go, before her husband came home and treated him to the butt-end of his whip.

By this time the poor ancient looked helpless and disconcerted. Everything about the house had changed. Where once the old easy chair had stood, a couch was now placed against the wall. The pewter had gone, but still there was sufficient to convince him that Nant Clwyd *was* Nant Clwyd. In a trembling voice and quailing manner he told her he had gone out yesterday morning to hunt, and how a heavy sleep had stolen upon him, so that he had passed the night in the woods.

" Ah ! " replied the shrew, " I have heard my husband say that there was once a rumour that his father was lost while hunting, and everybody thought he had been killed ! " Then she shook with anger, and again screamed at him to go away.

This roused the fury of the old stranger. He declared that Nant Clwyd *was* his house and he should insist upon his rights. Then, with a heavy crash, the door was slammed in his face, and the day seemed colder and more cheerless than before.

He turned his tottering steps towards the nearest farm, the homestead of his friend Caradog ; and there his eyes fell on an old, old man, helpless, and sitting thoughtfully by the sparkling fire-side. They talked in quavering tones about the youth and the days gone by, and, as they conversed, those days appeared like a fair summer scene in a

playhouse. Then the mist of the years rolled
away, and each knew even as he was known.
Their trembling old arms lay about each other's
neck, and unwonted tears trickled down their
furrowed cheeks. Then did Idwal learn his true
position; and the poor, old man found the society
of Caradog so kindly that he did not return to

" ALL THE OLD FOLK . . . WERE INVITED."

Nant Clwyd. A welcome meal (nay, call it a
feast) was spread upon the table, and all the old
folk of the neighbourhood were invited, and
came crowding to see the long-lost Idwal. The
evening hours sped by in a delightful manner.
They talked over old times till sleep grew more
welcome than words ; and then the two old men

withdrew to share the same room and bed, while silence spread over the household.

The following day, when all the others had come down, these two were so long in making their appearance that Caradog's kinsfolk went up to call them forth to breakfast. Yet no response was made to the loud rapping on the bedroom door. Then the family passed into the still and peaceful room, and there upon the bed the two old friends lay quiet and at rest. Death, the gentle friend of the aged, had come in the night, and, holding a hand of each, had wandered forth with Idwal and Caradog. Yet it was often said in the neighbourhood that it was not Idwal but his spirit which came to fetch his comrade, and as soon as Caradog had heard the message, fain at heart, he had begged the rulers of the land of Spirits that he might go forthwith with his comrade, and thus they had fared forth together to a better land.

But this is quite certain, a curse fell upon the family at Nant Clwyd, yea, even to the fifth generation. Do what they would everything was a failure. Seed-time and harvest brought every year their tale of disaster. It is true, moreover, that the farm was sold nine times before the curse departed off the fields that Idwal had tilled, and from the home to which he had brought his young bride. And that is the story of the deserted farmhouse in the valley of Nant Clwyd.

XII

MODRED THE DRUID

Long, long ago, when the all-conquering sword of Rome had pierced to the westernmost part of Britain, staining the green fields red with the glorious blood of her defenders, there lived a Druid named Modred Men called him Modred the wise, for he was known far and wide for his holiness, and wisdom, and his devotion to the gods. Yes, indeed, he was truly a worthy Druid ; but alas ! the times had swept evil days over his old age, and from henceforth his lot was to see the holy altars dripping with the blood of its godly priests, and the sacred groves mocked by the cruel dogs of war. So Modred sought for a shelter from the howling tempest, and wandered among the old, grey hills till he found what he sought.

The shelter he chose was a cave placed securely in the ample bosom of a broad mountain-side. A hidden and gentle slope led up to its entrance, and so winding and puzzling was the path that the cave was unknown to all save those whom the kindly hand of the Druid guided to the secret place. Within the cave there was room and to spare, for nature had separated it into several large divisions where one might find rest and comfort. And so this quiet, secluded spot was a haven for harmlessness and virtue. Hither came young and tender virgins fleeing from the passionate soldiery. Hither, also, virtuous women would flock from the cruelty of their foes; and the fatherless and widowed came to Modred's cave for safety and solace. Yes, and hither crept brave old warriors wounded in the fray, bringing their wounds to Modred to be healed. He nursed them with loving care and skill until, restored and healed, they departed with renewed strength to the field of battle.

Every morning and every evening Modred went out from his cave, and, bending low in an attitude of prayer, poured forth his worship amidst the holy oak-trees in the grove that stood in grandeur on the slopes of the mountain. Whether the lofty summits were veiled in the cold grey mist, or gleamed with the warm rays of the sun, whether the mountain thrilled with the song of a thousand streaming rivulets, or rose vast and silent in a mantle of silver snow—alike in all weathers, Modred bent before his country's gods. In the grove he built a holy altar, and, according to the custom of the wise and learned who had gone before him, he duly placed upon it the sacred offering of meal. Thus he passed his days in prayer, reflection, and almsgiving. He drank the water from a limpid brook that leaped clear as crystal from the rock where nature had shaped its crude cradle. His food was the health-giving herbs that grew in friendly profusion around that lonely abode.

Such was Modred the Druid, in whose daily life and custom were united the sinlessness of childhood and the wisdom of old age.

One day Modred had wandered afar to seek for healing herbs. The sun rode glittering in a clear, burnished sky. All nature stood in tuneful peace. Suddenly, as he walked, his eye caught sight of red stains that lay upon the herbage. As he went on, the red drops were spilled more freely, and his gentle heart called him to follow the scarlet stream to its source. In a spot tangled with undergrowth, and hedged round with thick tendrils, Modred found a man in armour lying stretched upon the ground. He seemed to have swooned, and, as the aged priest turned the limp head towards him, he saw that the warrior was in the flower of youth. His armour showed that he was a Roman, and, therefore, a relentless foe. Yet pity for the sorrowful and helpless swept through Modred's heart, causing him to forget forthwith the enemies that spread ruin and havoc over the land. He lifted him tenderly in his arms, and poured a cordial between the pale and parted lips. Then he gave the wounded man a herbal medicine that he always carried with him, and of such restorative power that a few drops of it seemed to give new life. The youth opened his eyes, and there came a sigh from the returning spirit, but he was still so weak and helpless that he could not stand upon his feet. Modred, seeing that the stranger could not rise without more help than he could give, hurried back, through the day's noontide heat, to his cave, and, ere long, returned with a youth named Gwydyr.[1]

Now Gwydyr was the bravest of all the youth of Britain who fearlessly bore the sword to defend their freedom, and he was as fair to behold as he was brave, for nature had formed his body in wondrous wise, and thus his appearance was such as art often refuses to the work of her most ardent disciples. Often had Gwydyr given proof of his courage in the battles he had fought against the enemy. His courtesy, also, matched his bravery, and his kindliness of heart was known to all.

With Gwydyr's help the wounded Roman youth was borne to the cavern ; but, because he was a Roman, they first bandaged his eyes, lest he might learn the approach to the hiding-place and in that way be the cause of future war.

So they brought him to the cave, removed the bandage, then, unlacing his armour, laid him upon a heap of soft and yielding moss. Modred

[1] Gwidir.

gave careful heed to the cruel slashes and found that with care the youth might soon be cured. He soothed the aching pain with oil, placed certain herbs of unfailing virtue upon the gaping wounds and then stole out, leaving him to the gentle care of soft and kindly sleep.

When he returned, after some lapse of time, the stranger youth was so recovered by reason of the medicine and the miraculous power of sleep, that he could ask Modred in a low and trembling voice into whose hands he had fallen. Then, indeed, when he learned that his captors were Britons, he showed by his expression that he had no hope of mercy from them. Modred read his face like an open book, and, knowing his thoughts, tried to dispel his fears and suspicion.

" Youth," said he, " thou art in the hands of those whom thy nation is apt to call wild people. Yet, though we are in truth strangers to those marvellous arts that are practised by civilized nations to lay a fair covering over the most wicked and treacherous intentions, believe me when I say that the Britons are not unfamiliar with the virtues of hospitality and courtesy. Yea, they love victory, but they never rejoice in the blood of a fellow-creature. Therefore, brave youth, know that whilst thou art in the care of Modred, thou shalt be safe from harm and all unkindness."

The young Roman greatly wondered at this unexpected beneficence; yet he could but think that this courteous behaviour was only to cloak some hostile intention. But as he was ready with Roman courage to meet his fate calmly and bravely, whether it smiled or frowned, he did not allow his surroundings to disturb his state of mind, and this, of course, was the best way to re-establish his health of body.

In the morning the Druid saw that his patient had wonderfully recovered, so they talked together. Modred learned that the young Roman was an officer in the invading army, and that accompanied by five soldiers he had left the camp about three days before. His aim had been to find out the position of his foes. But his men, so he thought, had been hired by some fellow-officer who had long had a grudge against him, and at the moment when, unsuspecting, his back was turned upon them, they, like traitors, had struck him down, leaving him as one who is dead. He thanked Modred for his kindness.

" Ay, aged priest, my heart goes out to thee in gratitude, nor can I ever hope to repay thee for thy timely aid."

As he spoke these words, there came upon their ears a rushing sound as of many voices. Modred, looking wistfully upon the youth, gave him a sign that he should follow him in silence from the cave. As they entered the great white light of the day, they saw that a number of people of all ages and kinds had gathered together for the rites of sacrifice.

12

At the appearance of Modred a hush spread over the multitude—but it was a hush that yielded like calm upon the sea before the lashing tempest. At the sight of the Roman youth a murmur arose, for each man turned to his neighbour in stern inquiry. Passion welled forth and spread hither and thither unrestrained. " Tear the accursed foe to pieces ! " they howled. Then they pressed forward up the dark slope of the hoary mountain. Nor did the gentle aspect of Modred check them ; and tragedy gazed out from behind her mask. Yet they stayed as Modred raised his aged arm and looked for silence.

" Brothers, sisters," he exclaimed, " have I so long served you that you thus invade my habitation ? Is the oil of anointing that I have poured into your wounds to be paid for in the warm red blood of my guest ? Is that your gratitude to your aged priest ? Is that your love for your country's religion ? "

Thus Modred was winning them, but an evil-faced old woman on the outskirts of the crowd screamed, " Down with the accursed foes who tear our children from our breasts and spill the fathers' blood upon the threshold. On, then, ye cravens, and kill ! Ay, and if need be, arise and slay the babbling old priest. The gods of Britain await the victim ye shall offer."

Then a groan of bitterness spread over the assembly, like the low moaning that passes through the swaying tops of the oak-trees when the storm comes from the west. Again the men, howling fiercely their hatred, moved forward and Modred knew he could not stay them. Nor could Gwydyr, eager though he was to save Modred's guest. He was brushed aside in the pathway as a stone is swept away by the rushing of the winter's snow when it seeks the valley.

" THE MEN . . . MOVED FORWARD."

Then came a sudden and wondrous hush over all the mountain-side. Morfudd,[1] sister of Gwydyr, lovely and pure as he was brave and handsome, came slowly down the pathway from the mountain-top. The trembling rays of the morning sun fell upon her snow-white garments. The breeze lifted very gently her blue-black

[1] Morvith.

hair as it streamed around her shoulders, and her throat was white as the flowers she carried in her hands.

"Lo!" the people cried. "Lo! the virgin of the sacrifice," and they knelt upon the soil. And Morfudd came gently down the pathway, and,

"THE VIRGIN OF THE SACRIFICE."

as she advanced, she sang with a sweet voice, like a bird singing its first love song in the groves at springtide :

> " Amid the silvery moonlight,
>   With golden sickle free,
> A virgin pure and sinless,
>   I cut thee from thy tree.

O vervain, fair and holy,
  I wreathe thee in my hands,
As white, and pure, and spotless
  As are thy sacred strands.

And now in love I cast thee,
  Fair pledge of heavenly peace,
Upon this wounded warrior
  That enmity may cease."

" THAT IS THE GRAVE OF MODRED."

Long years after, three people stood by the
Cave of Modred, and they placed vervain upon the
little heap of stones that stood at its entrance,
while at a distance four boys and two young girls
watched the older folk.

" Why do they do that ? " asked a tiny, black-haired maiden. " Why do father and mother and our Uncle Gwydyr look so sad ? "

And the eldest son of the Roman youth and Morfudd answered :

" Because that is the grave of Modred the Druid."

XIII

EINON AND OLWEN

On the slopes of the beautiful valley of Rhondda-wen, there lived many years ago a family who were as fair as the fairness of the spring dawn when the lingering snows fondle the distant hill-tops. Gentle and kindly were they; so gentle and so kindly, indeed, that even the swift swallows stayed to twitter around them, and the flowers waved softly as they passed. The family was for generations called the Fair Family. Would you like to know why? Read this story and you will understand.

Once upon a time, long years ago, a shepherd boy called Einon went out with his sheep upon the mountains. While he was there a dense mist tumbled out of the sky and fell like a great curtain upon the hills and valleys, so that before long the boy had lost his way, and was separated from his sheep. He wandered on and on until he came to a low-lying valley, damp and over-grown with long green rushes which formed strange circles. When the shepherd lad saw these rings, he remembered that people had told him about them, and the fairies who danced in and out, along the marsh. So he hurried away as fast as he could run to avoid meeting any of these creatures ; and he ran till the sweat rolled down his face and his breath came in choking sobs. But run as he would his feet seemed to make hardly any progress. His heart sank with despair.

Just then there came out of the mist, and from among the dank rushes, a small old man. At least, he seemed to be extremely old, yet his eyes were very merry and wonderfully blue.

" What is the matter, my boy ? " said he.

" I'm trying to find my way out of the valley because of the fairies," answered the lad.

" Oh ! " said the old man, " you had better come with me, then ; but come very silently, and pray don't speak a word until I say that you may do so."

So the shepherd boy followed his guide over craggy paths and through tangles of bushes, till at last they reached a large stone which stood upright in the ground. The old man tapped three times on this stone, and then, putting his wrinkled hand upon it, pushed it back, and lo ! before their very eyes opened a long, narrow passage, dipping down beneath the earth, and broken, every now and again, by little flights of stairs. And the wonder of it was that a grey light seemed to pour out of the stone walls and roof, and thus one could see quite plainly.

" Follow me," quoth the old man. " Fear nothing, for no harm shall come to you."

" THE OLD MAN TAPPED THREE TIMES."

The shepherd boy did not like to refuse, so he followed his nose, more like a dog going to be hanged than after the manner of a merry-hearted boy.

But soon he forgot his fears. A lovely country-side, filled with the flashing light of the sun, and decked with green trees spangled with golden fruit spread before him. Winding rivers gleamed in the sunshine, and on the rich slopes of the verdant hills stood many a magnificent palace wrought wonderfully of white stone which dazzled the sight. Through the verdure babbled noisy little brooks, dancing in glee round the soft-moulded hills. Birds with gorgeous plumage flitted by, like fleeting rainbows, and the bushes were decked with the brightness of a thousand lovely blossoms. The boy walked in silence, dumb with the sense of loveliness that stole over his nature. Then the scene changed. Gold and silver veins lay about the hills and rocks like sunbeams darting over the surface of a lake. Wonderful music from myriad instruments came wafted on the breeze. Yet he could see no one but his old, old guide.

Soon they sat down at a table spread with a banquet more than fit for a king. Course after course came unbidden, carried by unseen hands ; and, when they had eaten, then the dishes of their own accord passed away before their sight. Round about the shepherd boy stole sweet mur-murings. Soft whispers fell on his ears, gentle voices called him, but look as he might, he could see no one.

At last the old man spoke.

" Speak as much as ever you wish," said he.
" There's no need for silence now."

Then to the boy's wonder and alarm he realized
that he could not speak. His tongue seemed to
lie in his mouth like an icicle, so hard and so cold
it had become. His panic increased and he knew
not what to do—when, all at once, there appeared
(whence he could not tell) a plump old woman
with cheeks like rosy apples, and she smiled gently
at the lad. Behind her stole three fair maidens,
loveliest of the lovely, and still more lovely.
Their fair skin was like the hawthorn for its
whiteness, and the rose for its warmth. Long
golden hair streamed over their shoulders, falling
in ringlets round their waists. They glanced half
playfully at the wondering youth, and he longed
to speak to them; but he could not. His lips and
tongue refused to move. Then one of the maidens
came coyly towards him, twisting her fair curls
about her white fingers, and glancing downward
with her tender eyes. Lifting her warm red lips
she imprinted their glow upon the lad's chill
mouth, and at once his ice-cold tongue grew soft
and yielding, just as the kiss of spring sets free
the ice-bound streams of the mountain-side.

Under the spell of her kiss he seemed to live in
a glorious paradise. He spoke freely and with
joyousness. His fear fell from him like a garment,
and he paid no heed to time. The days slipped
by till a year and a day had passed, only, to the

shepherd lad, the time seemed to be but one day, fair and bright with never a cloud.   At last came the remembrance of his home, and as the thought

" BEHIND HER STOLE THREE FAIR MAIDENS."

came to him, *hiraeth* stirred in his breast—that pain which clutches the heart when one is far away from the dear old home of one's childhood.

He ran to the old man, and, thanking him earnestly for all his kindness, begged that he might go and visit his friends once again.

" Wait a spell," he answered, " and you shall go."

And so it happened. But when the lad came to the moment of his departure, Olwen (for that was the name of the maiden who kissed him) was sad at heart. Tear-drops stood in her soft, blue eyes and her lips trembled ; and Einon's heart grew cold within him at the thought of saying good-bye to her.

Still he felt he must go, so they gave him gold and silver, rich jewels without number, and he made his journey to his long-lost home. In great glee he came to his native village, thinking of the welcome he would receive, but sad to tell, people looked at him and wondered who he was.

" *That*, the shepherd lad who was killed by his mate on the mountain-side ! Why he's not in the least like him. Besides, the other shepherd fled because he had killed him."

Even his own father and mother did not remember him. Nor was this to be wondered at, for Einon had gone away just a poorly clad shepherd boy, but now he stood among them dressed in rich apparel, splendid in manner and speech, and possessed of riches untold.

" 'Tis some strange and noble lord," they said, " Einon was poor."

Well, Einon dwelt with his people till he felt his heart yearning for the tender glances of Olwen, and one Thursday night when the silver moon was full, and flooding the deep blue sky, he stole away again, none knowing whither he had gone.

Great was the rejoicing in the underworld when Einon came back, and none was more blithe then Olwen. The absence had made their hearts more loving, and they longed to be married that they might never be separated again. This was a great difficulty, for in the underworld nothing was more disliked than noise and confusion. At last, however, as it were half secretly and in great peacefulness, Einon and Olwen were united, and in perfect happiness they lived together in the silent, gleaming underworld.

Then, some time after, once again, there came that stirring wish in Einon's heart—the call of home came over the silence, and through the gleam ; and he felt he must obey the call. With great difficulty, and many earnest words, he won the permission of the old and merry-eyed man. He was allowed to carry his fair bride with him. When all was ready the merry-eyed old man led forward two white mules. Indeed, they were so white that in hue they were more like snow than anything else, a d on these lovely creatures Einon and Olwen came to the old home.

Much as the people admired the grandeur of Einon they were even more struck with the beauty of Olwen.

" Never before was there such beauty on earth," said one.

" The sun never looked down on such loveliness," exclaimed another.

" EINON AND OLWEN CAME TO THE OLD HOME."

And everyone paid tribute to her wonderful and shapely form.

Time passed by and a child was born to the happy pair, and they called him Taliesin. The whole village, yea, indeed all the other villages round about, reverenced Einon and Olwen, for their riches were immense and their heritage was truly marvellous. But there was one thing which cast a shadow. About this time people thought that they would like to know the descent of Einon's wife.

" Whose daughter is she ? " said they. " It is only right that everyone should have a family tree."

So they came to Einon and asked him who his wife was, but Einon would not say.

" Then," quoth an old wiseacre, " she must be one of the Fair Family." (Tylwyth Têg.)

" Yes, indeed," said Einon. " There is no question about that. She is of a very fair family. She has two sisters even more fair than she. To see them together, in the open day, is to see the sunshine ripple over the cornfield, and the blushing blossoms of spring leap at once from the pure winter snow. If you but saw them, you would say they were indeed a fair family ! "

So spake Einon, and from that day the wonderful family was called " The Fair Family."

XIV

THE GATE-KEEPER OF GWENT

In the days of Gwyddno-Garan hir, son of the King of Gwent, who was the son Macsen, there lay a wide tract of land where now roll the waters of Cardigan Bay. That time was more than fifteen hundred years ago, before the troubles which fell upon the Cymry [1] with the coming of the Saxons, and in the years when our heroes and our singers had not as yet felt the heavy blows of the enemy from over the sea.

Gwyddno-Garan hir, or Gwyddno Long Shank, was a mighty prince, ruling in the Lowland Hundred over a people who were his loving subjects. Not only was he great in body, but in mind and speech was he also great ; for he made poems which are famous to this day, and they were sung to the harp, and so passed into the language and song of the people of his realm, who rejoiced in a prince so mighty in war and skilful in the battle of words.

There is one poem written by Gwyddno-

[1] Kimrĕ.

13   177

Garan hir which tells of the terrible misfortune that befell his land in the days of his princedom. It is, perhaps, the greatest of his works, for it sprang from his heart when the tears of sorrow were in his eyes. Over the wide river of years, the song tells us, man is born to trouble, just as the sparks fly upward. We hear its sad message wailing over the centuries that have fled; and, as we listen to its throbbing notes, our hearts beat in sympathy with that prince who lived so long ago, and we sorrow for his subjects who woke suddenly one day to an agony of affliction and loss. So universal is sorrow in all lands, and in all ages, that the measure of Gwyddno's song cannot fail to awaken echoes of regret as we catch the far-off notes that issued from a stricken heart —a song which has given rise to our proverb: "The sigh of Gwyddno-Garan hir when the waves swept over his land"; a song that is wafted through the still air of the evening when the bells of Aberdovey from beneath the sea scatter tidings of a land that once revelled in the light of heaven and rejoiced in the warmth of the sun.

The realm of Gwyddno was fruitful, abounding in all the fair gifts of nature, who, from her gentle hands, scattered fruit and flower over the fertile soil. Who, indeed, has never heard of the sixteen cities of Cantref y Gwaelod,[1] and of the

[1] Gwȳlod.

wonderful fishing basket of Gwyddno ? Such a basket in itself spoke of the abundance that prevailed. Why, if food for a single person were placed within it, the next time the lid was opened sufficiency for a hundred was discovered ; so that this famous receptacle became known, far and wide, as one of the rareties of kingly regalia in Britain.

In the orchards, when spring awakened in the early months of the year, the trees burst into a wealth of fragrant blossoms that in a tender and kindly climate mellowed into the fruits of summer. And, as the trees donned their gay robes of pink and red and white, so, over the fields, flowers opened in the light of the lengthening days to welcome the return of the sun. Breezes from the west played mirthfully over the country-side, breathing upon young leaves and blossoms life-giving virtue, and wafting abroad the melodies of spring, who desires all her children to be happy and rejoice in her presence.

In such a fruitful land plenty was enjoyed by great and small. Food and wine and mead were the bountiful gifts of Nature ; for the crops flourished year by year in the rich soil ; the vines sheltered among their leaves grapes that yielded the generous wines of autumn ; bees, which found such a treasure of honey in the sweet summer flowers, stored in their hives the harvest of busy hours of toil and the full glory of the life-giving sun ; so that man, in the darkness of winter, might have draughts of mead to cheer his heart. Can we wonder that, in such glad surroundings, these people sang, and danced, and welcomed life ? Nature meant her children to be joyful, and, for that reason, she showers her gifts upon the earth. Alas ! that man should have thwarted her generous will, and, by placing his own greedy purposes before all, have dragged his brothers into dearth and drudgery ! The days of the past have seen sorrow ; but, verily, man was not always tied by the cords that have been woven through the centuries by the cunning of the powerful.

Yet, in this land of song and mirth, where man lived so easily, and fed from the bounty of nature's open hands, one menace hung for ever over the heads of the subjects of Gwyddno-Garan hir as a heavy cloud will hover over the brow of a lofty mountain, threatening the valleys with its burden.

The country lay so low that only by constant effort could the ravages of the ocean be warded from the fertile fields. For generations past the great sea had groaned at the edge of the land like some fierce and hungry monster, who, with patient cunning, lies in wait for a victim he seeks to devour. Yet so skilful is man, so triumphant amid the tremendous forces of the universe, that he employs his puny strength to thwart their hostile purposes. To protect their sixteen cities the people of this realm had built great dykes, which proclaimed by day and night to the sea : " Hitherto shalt thou come, but no further." So that the land endured, and was the home of content and safety. When the tide was low the sea made no threat ; but when, at the bidding of the deep, the waters were loosened, and came rolling higher and higher, men knew that their enemy must be controlled. For this reason at the river mouths, where the streams rippled forth to mingle their waters with the heaving ocean, people had placed great gates, cunningly fashioned, so that when the sea retreated they might be opened, for man and beast to issue forth ; but, when the murmur of the sea arose and waves began their threatening march towards the low-lying territory, these guardian gates were closed, as doors are closed against night and winter. Thus through the years the enemy beat vainly against man's skilful barriers.

Now, so important was this office of opening and closing the gates, upon which depended the very lives of the people, as well as the safety of the land, that it was regarded by all as one of the greatest of trusts, to be placed only in the charge of men of character and proved experience. For this reason, the Kings of the realm had ever striven with diligence to choose those who should act as the guardians of the race, and stand like sentinels at the outskirts of a camp, to challenge all who came unbidden to the boundaries. Various men had filled this great office, and in the course of nature had passed into that long sleep which drops at last upon all the children of man. But, for many years before the days of Gwyddno-Garan hir, the serious charge of opening and shutting the gates had rested in the hands of one family, who, from father to son, had passed down the duty of protecting their trusting fellows from the cruel sea.

It was into this family that Seithenyn was born, so that from childhood he grew up in sight and knowledge of the gates. Day by day he saw his father, at the proper times, go from their home and superintend the closing of the barriers. At first he watched this from his mother's arms ; then he would toddle of his own accord to the doors when his father went upon his duty. As time advanced and Seithenyn grew in stature, the day arrived that saw him walk proudly at his father's side, feeling that he himself was, in some measure, associated with this noble work of debarring from their joyous world that direful foe which for ever lay in wait for their lives. Thus he was trained and inured to the duties that were to be his own when his father was too aged to fulfil them any longer.

Among these joyful people Seithenyn grew to be a happy and beloved youth. His high birth brought him into touch with the greatest and

wealthiest of the land ; he was known and esteemed
by the Prince himself, and many a day and many
a night did they pass together, hunting, singing

" HE WOULD TODDLE TO THE DOORS."

and enjoying the gifts of life in the golden days
of youth. Seithenyn was skilful at song ; his
hand was strong and sure with weapons of every
kind ; his foot was swift as the foot of the roe

upon the mountain-side. His face was ruddy as the rowan berry, and his hair black as a raven's wing. His eyes flashed like the lightning as it glitters through the clouds upon the mountain crests ; or, again, they glowed with a light as gentle as the early dawn of some clear summer day. No one could help loving Seithenyn ; but, indeed, therein lay his danger, and the danger of the whole country.

It came to pass when Seithenyn was only a young man that his father, riding one day from the chase, was flung from his horse, and killed. That night, Seithenyn himself, with tears streaming from his eyes, went forth, and, for the first time in his life, closed the gates and saw that all was safe. The next day also he fulfilled the duty ; and so he continued till his father was laid to rest beneath the earth. What then was more natural that to him, in his early manhood, should fall the duty that had for so long a time been handed down in his family from father to son—the duty which his own eyes had seen accomplished ever since they could look with intelligence, the duty which now for days he himself had carefully fulfilled ? Men said, nay Gwyddno-Garan hir himself said, " He is his father's son. Young though he be, yet duty lies upon him as naturally as day dawns upon the smiling earth. Let the task be his, and may he, in his turn, hand down the duty, well accomplished, to the son who succeeds him."

So Seithenyn took the keys of office and assumed in early manhood the responsibility of protecting all the people from the danger that lay beyond the dykes.

" CLOSED THE GATES. . . ."

Having thus speedily reached such a high position, Seithenyn was more courted than ever before. All his natural charms were now enhanced by the authority that came to him with his advancement. He was sought after, praised, entertained and admired by all, but especially by the maidens of the realm, who, one and all, desired to be his wife.

It was not to be wondered at that Seithenyn was spoiled in many ways by the flattery that came with such persistence ; so that, missing the discipline of hardship and strife which is the lot of most youths, he formed habits that were only too likely to lead to the weakening of his character. Unfortunately, these habits were numerous, but two were especially to be dreaded. One was that he yielded far too readily to the lure of woman's winning tongue ; the other was that, amid revelry and dance, he learned to quaff too deeply of wine and mead, and to love the glow which these liquids brought into mind and body.

These habits, at first scarcely to be noticed, at length grew to such a degree that people began to talk about them. Seithenyn was now a handsome man, and, by reason of his office, powerful in the realm ; but he was no longer the attractive, open youth whom people had loved so much. Moreover, the days of single life had ended. He had chosen for his wife the daughter of a nobleman of high position, and because he was no longer eligible, interest has ceased to centre round him ; so that instead of praise and admiration, criticism and blame were levelled against his reputation. But Seithenyn cared for none of these things. He had the love of Gwyddno-Garan hir, and was secure at the Court.

It would have been better for him, it would have been better for everyone, if this had not been so. But, as it was, fearing neither loss of office nor loss of esteem, Seithenyn, as the years rolled by, became confirmed in his evil ways, until at last the gate-holder, the protector of men's lives, the one man upon whom rested the safety of the most beautiful lands of Wales, the Cantref y Gwaelod, was known far and wide as a drunkard. As a drunkard he was spoken about in the streets ; as a drunkard his name was whispered at the Court ; and as a drunkard his name was sung in the songs of Wales. Nor was that all. There are degrees even in evil. At last Seithenyn stood forth as one of the three arch-drunkards in the Isle of Britain, and as such he is known to this day in the songs that have come down to us.

And this was the man who watched over the dykes ! How strange is human nature, and how powerful in days gone by has been the influence of birth and rank ! In that realm there were hundreds of men who could have been trusted to guard the gates ; but because Seithenyn was his father's son, and a friend of the Prince, no man dared to suggest that his drunkenness was a peril to the lives of the people. Besides, the years went by, and no harm had ever come ; so that at last people ceased to trouble. We become accustomed to joy as well as to sorrow, the bright days of summer and the darkness of winter. Loss and danger, in the first instance so grievous, so galling, become in the progress of time customary fetters.

The years fled and were gathered into the treasury of the ages, and now the last of the happy seasons had come to the people of Gwyddno-Garan hir ; but they knew it not. It is just like that in life. We tread its paths according to our custom, until one day, to our surprise, the journey ends altogether unexpectedly, and we marvel at the change. Thus spring yields to summer, summer to autumn, autumn to winter, and the flight of the year is over.

A great feast was held in the realm over which Seithenyn kept such strange watch and ward, a feast that marked the gathering in of the harvest of fruit and corn. Every autumn, when the garners were full to bursting, this feast was celebrated ; for men rejoiced to know they had respite from toil in the field, and possessed stores to carry them through the dark months of winter. From the humblest cottager to the Prince himself this feeling of gladness ran freely, and men were wont to assemble at the feast to laud those who had gathered in the wealth that was scattered so abundantly in their midst.

Everyone rejoiced in these days of autumnal mellowness. Men, women, and children danced, sang, and were merry. Wine and mead flowed freely, and it was good to live at such a time. The sharp sickles, bright with usage, were hung in the barn ; harps resounded loud and shrill, the feet of dancers twinkled to their music.

And where was Seithenyn upon whom all depended for their lives ? Where was Seithenyn, the Guardian of the Gate and one of the three arch-drunkards of Britain ? When all were merry and careless, and resting from toil and care, Seithenyn should have been at his post, more zealous, more earnest, as his father and father's father had ever been at such seasons. But the heat of mead and the glow of wine had melted the heart of Seithenyn so that virtue had oozed from his soul, and he joined lustily in the revelry and the drinking that were the order of the day. And while he drank deeply, and yet more deeply as the singers and dancers filled the air with merriment, the gates were neglected.

A great round moon was shedding her solemn beauty upon the fields ; and the streets in the villages were bright as at noonday. The glow from the houses looked dusky red against this flood of radiance ; and sounds of revelry were flung back from the vast silence of the world of nature, as though man's works were an affront to the majesty that surrounded him. Both silence and light seemed to implore man to kneel and pray, whereas his song and dance rather proclaimed

his indifference to the grandeur of night. Away
on the dykes the moonlight fell upon desolation,
making the sand whiter still, so that the shadows
of the marram grass lay like little black streaks,
left by the footsteps of the banished darkness.
Over the sea where the tide had risen, glory
streamed in its fullest splendour, tingeing the
crests of waves, and spreading like meshes of
molten gold over the restless waters. But somehow that night a sound which was not usually
present rose from the ocean, a sound as of fulness
and power beyond words to utter. As though
deep were calling unto deep, this voice of the
night waxed stronger and stronger, calling, but
in vain, for man to watch, even if he did not pray
(although, perchance, to pray is to watch), lest
he be overwhelmed in some moment of weakness.
For now, in the time of full moon, the waters
were heaping themselves together, and, at this
moment, there was urgent need for the closing
of the gates to resist the vanguard of that hostile
army, which advanced with banners tossing and
heaving, where the golden crested waves rolled
mightily towards the shore.

And Seithenyn was lying, intoxicated, in the
royal palace of the Prince.

Higher rose the tide, and louder boomed the
voice of the waves. At the very foot of the dykes
foamed and hissed a volume of water such as man
had rarely seen. The gates that should have

been closed were open. The word that should have been broadcast throughout the realm was locked, for ever, silent in a drunkard's heart. Where reason and fear, vigour and resolution should have been man's weapon on this night of silent beauty, careless song, heedless dance, and, at last, drunken orgy unnerved the body and rendered impotent the brain ; and ever the waves rose higher.

Then, towards dawn, some who were roaming by chance, saw in the light of the waning moon, blended with the red flush of coming day, the horror that hung upon their land. Round the sides of the dykes flooded the swirl of waters, and at that sight a quavering sob of terror stole from the throats of those who looked. Then, as if by instinct, a cry ran trembling, here and there, wherever men were sufficiently sober to understand the calamity that this new day was to pour upon their lives. " Where is Seithenyn ? " " Where is Seithenyn ? " " Why are the gates open ? " Such questions were scattered upon the air. But no answer came ! Then someone said, foolishly, " Let us shut the gates ! " But who can brush aside the might of the ocean ? When a few men tried to close the great wooden gates, they were swept from their feet, and borne like straws upon the surface of a swift running river.

And now all the land awoke to horror. Men,

women and children, looking towards the dykes, saw the fiendish heads of the waves as they leapt like madmen and tossed their foam right over the broad banks of sand. Dawn became overcast, and dark clouds hung lowering in the sky. Gwyddno-Garan hir, summoned from his royal palace, came swiftly, with hair streaming in the wind, to see the line of black waters crash swiftly into foam and fury as they poured round the barriers. He looked and uttered the same cry, " Where is Seithenyn ? " Then he turned and shouted, " Save yourselves, the dykes will soon be down."

Forthwith arose a panic such as was never seen before, save when God let loose His deluge upon the face of the earth. A host of people, ever increasing in number and volume, rushed from cottage, from hamlet, from village, in search of dear life, and leaving property as a worthless thing. The revelry of the night suddenly died before this awful fear, and, with blanched faces and frantic steps, human beings fled for safety, and in their haste trod one another under foot. And still the waves leapt higher over the dykes, till at last, all along the line of the coast, the sandbanks broke and melted into the breast of the ocean, as a huge wall of water burst with a bellowing boom over the realm of Gwyddno-Garan hir.

For a while the eye could behold, here and there, forms of living beings. Now one saw a woman's hair floating like seaweed in the hissing foam ; again one saw a little child tossed backwards and forwards like a plaything in the power of evil beasts ; then a man swimming while strength endured, till, exhausted, he flung his arms to the threatening sky, and sank for ever. Long before mid-day, wherever the eye could reach, gleamed one lone waste of heaving waters.

Gwyddno-Garan hir was among those who escaped to Ardudwy, and he sat with a few breathless companions upon the slopes of Snowdon, gazing sorrowfully at the sea that lay over the Cantref y Gwaelod. Tears poured down his face, and, reaching out his hand, he took a harp that some reveller had carried, unheedingly, from the place where men and women had danced and sung together. And Gwyddno-Garan hir began to sing of the sorrow of the dawn, and the bitterness of despair ; how affliction burst suddenly upon mirth and beauty, and the comfort of the sparkling bowl ; how pride was banished by destruction :—

> " On Gwyddno's plains, see where the ocean strives !
>   Waste is the heritage my kinsmen brought.
> Come forth, Seithenyn, drinker of mens' lives !
>   Come, and behold the ruin thou hast wrought ! "

And as he sang these words, one of the company, starting to his feet, cried suddenly, " Lo ! What is that ? "

14

They all turned at these words and looked. Then Gwyddno-Garan hir saw that the waters

" SEITHENYN . . . WAS PASSED FROM CREST TO CREST."

were bearing something towards the land ; and as he gazed, he shuddered, for the evil of the thing was abhorrent to his eyes. As though the triumphant waves scorned its presence, as though the waters rejected its company, the body of Seithenyn, the arch-drunkard, was passed from crest to crest, and, as each wave handed it towards the shore, the water seemed to shudder at the contact and roll back swiftly to the open sea. Thus nearer and nearer drew the corpse, nearer to the feet of Gwyddno-Garan hir, nearer to the afflicted presence of those who alone were left of the race which his baseness had destroyed.

XV

THE FAIRY RINGS

THE snow-capped hills in the distance had lost
their dazzling whiteness. Winter was a thing of
the past, for now it was the season of soft perfumed
blossom, and the white hawthorn shone in the
hedgerows. Sheltered from winds and open to
the south, spring came speedily and with a gentle
softness in those upland valleys. All nature was
in a tender and smiling mood, like a young bride
seeking her lover's caresses.

But Nature's smiles were in no way reflected
in the face of Idris Abowen as he walked on the
sunlit terrace in front of Neuadd Hen. Not a
single tender note could be heard in his voice as
he cried angrily : " The plough shall wipe them
out ; the plough shall wipe them out. It shall
be done to-morrow at sunrise." And as he spoke,
his hand pointed with menacing forefinger at a
distant spot in the green meadow below.

A glance in that direction revealed a curious
fact. Three rings could be easily distinguished,
two smaller ones touching a larger one and the

whole forming a kind of double eight. There was no doubt whatever about it, for the grass of these rings was of a brighter green, and more beautiful by far, than the green that carpeted the rest of the meadow. As far back as the memory of man could travel these rings had been there. Famous poets of long ago had sung of them in the twenty-four metres of the awdl. These were the fairy rings of the Bendith y Mamau.[1] Everybody in the district knew that. Could one not hear their sweet music at eventide when the sun had set, and when the soft breeze stole out of the arms of the south ? Did not the hearts of men and maids who dwelt at Neuadd Hen overflow with hiraeth and unspoken longing when they listened to this mystic music ?

But, for Abowen, all this was but a hindrance to work, and on this particular occasion he was in a fury of annoyance. Bendith y Mamau had been singing their sweetest songs on the previous evening, and, rightly or wrongly, the master of Neuadd Hen attributed the lethargy of man and maid to this haunting melody that swept up the valley from those vivid rings in the meadow.

Abowen was a bold man and full of courage. On many occasions he had meditated drastic action. Yet, hitherto, some unseen influence had always stayed his hand. Now the vision of granaries filled in the autumn possessed his

[1] Bendith e Mamei, blessing of the mothers.

grasping soul. " To garner in autumn one must sow in spring," said he to himself. " The melodies of Bendith y Mamau must not hinder work. The meadow with the fairy rings has never felt the ploughshare. This year it shall produce what it has never produced before ; it shall yield wealth in its most glorious form, namely, in corn, golden corn."

As his mind pictured the field with its rustling, waving ears, his anger fell at the very thought of it, and he was silently glad. But he who sows should not rejoice as one who reaps and gathers in.

Early on the following morning the ploughs were ready and the oxen yoked. By the close of day the fairy circles had totally disappeared. Brown furrows had obliterated every trace of them, and in that field, for a time at least, Nature wore a sober livery.

A glorious summer followed. The crop in the field which had borne the fairy rings was the richest, the heaviest and the most beautiful of the whole estate, and the spirit of Idris Abowen rose at the promise of granaries bursting with their golden store.

Yet while he rejoiced at the idea of gain, others felt the sadness of a grievous loss. They regretted the absence of the soft, sweet music of the Bendith y Mamau ; for, now that it had ceased, they realized to the full the restful comfort which it had brought on still summer evenings, when the long day's work was over, and the heart craved for solace and love.

The summer wore away ; the evenings grew shorter ; and now it was early autumn. The household of Neuadd Hen had gone to bed for the night. Only one person remained up, and that was the master. He was sitting by the dull embers of the hearth, thinking over markets and prices, when there broke upon his ear a strange sound as of mocking laughter. He turned rapidly, but no one was in the room. Again the sound reached him, and now he opened the door and stepped upon the terrace overlooking the fields below. There he beheld a curious sight. Almost as he turned his eyes upon the field of his pride and hope, he saw a puff of smoke rise from the spot where once had been the fairy rings. The puff rose upwards. Then came another, then another, and puff followed puff, till over the whole field lay a sheet of white haze that shimmered in the pale light of the moon. Abowen stood and stared in amazement, but his silence soon yielded to a cry of horror, for now he discerned, darting through the smoke, sharp tongues of living fire, and almost before he could give the alarm his glorious field of corn was one mighty blaze that lit up the whole valley. The roar of it was awful to hear. People in the homesteads around were terrified, and flew in haste to the hill-tops. To make the work of destruction more terrible, suddenly a strong wind arose and roared down the valley throughout the night, till, at dawn, it was succeeded by the dismal hush of rain as it beat upon the alders. When the sun rose, its light fell upon a scene of pitiful desolation. The field of the fairy circles was black, yet, strange to say, it was the only one that had been swept by fire.

It is difficult to imagine the effect of this calamity on the master of Neuadd Hen. Suddenly it had been revealed to his soul that he had been guilty of an evil deed. Just to satisfy his own avarice he had destroyed what was beautiful and fair. That was why this punishment had fallen heavily upon him; and it was in this mood that he wandered through the lanes one autumn evening soon after the fire. So deeply was he plunged in thought that he failed to notice he was not alone. It was only when he heard a voice, clear as a bell, that Abowen became aware that anyone was present other than himself.

The voice said, " I am sent by my Pendefig to tell you that your sorrows are only just beginning."

The speaker was small, and by the brilliant moonlight Idris Abowen could see that he was richly but quaintly dressed. His face showed resolution, and he spoke with the quiet dignity of one who had suffered an unmerited wrong.

In his left hand he held a spear made of polished flint mounted on a shaft of hazelwood. He leaned on this while he was speaking.

" My people were once masters of all this country-side," said he, with a sweeping movement of his right hand. " We were happy and did no wrong. Then came your race and drove us away. You now deny us the right to a few yards of a meadow that once was entirely ours. The cruel heart that drove the ploughshare through the fairy circles shall surely be punished. So speaks my Pendefig." And he vanished.

With his mind still suffering from the shock of his recent disaster, Abowen did not for a moment realize the full menace of these quietly spoken words. The circumstances were so strange —the little man, his quaint appearance. But at last he understood. Instances of the Bendith y Mamau relentlessly in pursuit of vengeance flashed across his mind. And as he thought, his knees became as wax beneath him, and he sank to the ground sobbing bitterly like a child. Curious to relate the first words that passed his lips were those of the " Pader," taught to him when he was a little child. Thus do words thoughtlessly learned in our infancy come back to us in days of trouble, but they return fraught with solace and conviction.

The messenger of Bendith y Mamau could not have gone far, for when Idris Abowen lifted his eyes, he was standing a little distance off along the lane with his glance upon the humble figure of the praying man. He said nothing, but his face no longer wore the stern expression of a few moments earlier. Making a gesture with the

" STANDING A LITTLE DISTANCE OFF."

hazelwood shaft of his weapon, he disappeared again.

When Abowen rose to his feet, he no longer felt that black burden of impending evil. It seemed to him that, however great the punishment, it would no longer be more than his soul could bear. In such a chastened mood he returned home, and retired that night to rest.

The next evening, in the same spot, and at the very same hour, he met the messenger of the fairies once again.

He himself opened the conversation with these words : " Tell me, I pray you, what my punishment will be."

The tiny man, speaking in a calm and steady voice, replied : " My Pendefig is not swift to anger. He reads the hearts of men, and by your tears you have availed much. You shall not be punished, neither shall your children after you. The punishment will fall upon your descendants in the fourth generation."

And again, before another word could be uttered, he vanished suddenly, and Idris Abowen saw him no more.

Spring came, and the fairy circles in the large meadow by the river were greener and more beautiful than formerly, as though the fire had refined the garb of nature. Sweet music floated through the golden haze of the evenings, and its melodies were even sweeter than before. Yet now, the Master of Neuadd Hen, a chastened being, found solace in the gentle strains. People said that he paid visits to the fields on summer nights to be present at the fairy gatherings ; nay, it was asserted afterwards that he continued to do so until the end of his days.

All things change, but they change slowly in those Welsh valleys. The generation of Idris Abowen fell, one by one, almost as unmarked as the snowflakes fall upon ground already white with their fellows; and other generations followed that of Idris Abowen. The families of these successive sons of time lived in the homesteads scattered about the valleys. Now and again, youths, in a spirit of high adventure, would follow the river down to the plain, and visit great cities. A few of them returned with minds disillusioned.

> " A-roving, a-roving,
>   I'll go no more a-roving ;
>   Roving's been my ruin ;
>   I'll now stay here and dream."

Thus they would sing as they sat by the fire in the inglenook, or as they wandered about their pleasant valleys.

Among those who had returned was the young and handsome heir of Neuadd Hen, Arawn Abowen, the descendant of Idris Abowen in the fourth generation. That fact signified nothing to him, nor to anyone else. The Bendith y Mamau had departed. Their sweet strains were no longer heard. The threat of four generations had been long forgotten and the fairy circles in the meadow by the river had utterly disappeared.

It was a fine summer evening. From the wisps of sweet-scented hay lying in the lanes or hanging from the hedgerows, it was clear that the grass had been cut and built into ricks. Young folk from the neighbouring homesteads were leisurely crossing the fields, and their merry laughter rang through the stillness of evening. The girls in all the comeliness of youth, health and beauty, and daintily dressed in summer attire, were accompanied by young men. Some carried crythau (fiddles), and some harps. One and all turned towards Neuadd Hen.

A year and a day had gone by since the return of Arawn, and this evening they were to celebrate his betrothal to Gwenhwyfar, the heiress of Maesgwyn.[1] The large hall of the Neuadd, which had often in former days resounded to the warlike declamation of bards, amid the glitter of steel, was this night full of the sound of dancing and of song. It was when the music was merriest that the company became aware of a small and queerly dressed figure standing on the oak table by the open window. How long she had been there, none could tell. No one had seen her enter, but suddenly, and all at once, everyone looked at her.

She was dressed in a tight-fitting robe of purple and green, and her jet-black hair was gathered in a net studded with sparkling diamonds. On her tiny feet were sandals curiously wrought,

[1] Micegwin, the white meadow.

and of the colour of pure gold.   She was a fairy.
If there could have been any doubt as to that,
it was removed completely by the hazel wand
that she carried in her right hand.

"SHE WAS A FAIRY."

"What do you want here, you witch?" cried
one of the company, who had been drinking more
freely than the others.

"You do wrong to fix on me, or on any of my

people, that offensive name," boldly answered the little lady.

" I know you to be one by the wood of the wand you are holding," continued he.

" Know, then, man," was her reply, " that I am one of the Bendith y Mamau. We owned this fair land, which you now call yours, ages before your people came to dispossess us. It was from us that you learned the gentle arts of poetry and song. Yet, on every occasion you have used that cursed metal iron to harry us, knowing full well that its mere touch meant death to us. Have you not shod your oxen with it to trample upon us ? Have you not forged weapons of iron to slay us ? You have ripped the very soil of the meadows, our playgrounds, with implements fashioned from it. And now I am here to tell you that the time is ripe for avenging these wrongs ! "

" Witch ! " hissed the one who alone of all the company had been bold enough to speak. And as he spoke, he lunged forward to strike.

Quick as an arrow's flight the fairy moved forward. She touched with the slender wand the right shoulder of her assailant. It was but a touch, but the man's uplifted hand fell heavily to his side, paralysed ! Then, casting a last look over the company, the tiny visitant disappeared through the open window.

Except for a moan from the stricken man no one uttered a sound. He, like the others, stood gazing at the open window ; but his was the look of a gaping, hopeless paralytic, doomed for the rest of his days to turn in his mind thoughts which his tongue was powerless to utter.

From outside came wafted on the evening breeze strange harmonies, now sweet and low, now rising to notes of shrill defiance. These lasted far into the night, and were heard by the company as they dispersed and made their solemn way homeward through the fields and across the valley. The last to leave was Gwenhwyfar. The reassuring presence and tender words of Arawn, who accompanied her, helped to soothe her spirits and calm her fears. He saw her to her home, and then left her ; but he did not return that night to his own abode in Neuadd Hen. Days went by and weeks lengthened into months, but not a word of comfort or hope came to the distracted maiden. She would wander in the fields of Neuadd Hen, " the very soul of sad soliloquy," crying ever and again :

> " Hir yw'r dydd,
>   A hir yw'r nos,
>   A hir yw aros, Arawn." [1]

And not long afterwards she died of a broken heart and was laid to rest in the churchyard.

> [1] " Long is the day,
>   Long is the night,
>   And long 'tis waiting, Arawn."

Yet her gentle spirit still wandered over the fields. This, people knew full well ; for, constantly, they heard the sweet moaning of her voice, singing :

> " Hir yw'r dydd,
> A hir yw'r nos,
> A hir yw aros, Arawn."

One evening, after long years had passed away, and people were beginning to forget the story of Arawn and Gwenhwyfar, the family at Neuadd Hen were about to retire for the night when they heard a knock at the door. It was opened, and a tall and handsome stranger appeared. He said that he had come a long distance, and was weary. For this reason he begged for hospitality till the morning. The new-comer spoke with a strange accent and carried himself with a gentle and courteous bearing. The family bade him enter, and they made him welcome. The lady of the house, however, who spoke first, said : " The maids have gone to rest, and we have no room prepared. . . ." Then she paused. But, after glancing at her husband, she added in a faltering voice, " except one which is ever in readiness." Then, once again, she hesitated. The handsome stranger somehow seemed to understand what she had in her mind, for he bowed courteously, and said with a sad smile, " Sweet slumber, a weary wanderer, and a clear conscience."

15

Supper was laid for him, and, while he was eating, the daughter of the house entertained

" HE . . . SEATED HIMSELF AT THE HARP."

him with music on the harp, as was the custom in those days in Wales. They chatted together, and when the hostess paused, as if in search of a name by which to address him:

" I am called Arawn," he said simply.

At this they all started uneasily. By now, however, the visitor was oblivious of everything. He sat staring fixedly into the glowing embers. Waking from his reverie with a sigh, he arose, and, without uttering a word, seated himself at the harp. For a few moments he simply caressed its strings with his fingers lovingly, humming to himself, as if trying to recall a forgotten melody. Then his voice rang in clear and mellow tones, and there was that in it which told of the infinite sadness of years of pent-up sorrow.

The family of Neuadd Hen were renowned for their musical talent which had passed down to them for generations, and had produced two poets of real greatness. At first their mood was critical; but soon this gave place to deep emotion. Their very attitude showed this—the father and son seated at the large table with their foreheads resting on their hands; the mother and daughter standing with faces bathed in tears. It was only when the singer's voice rose to a climax with the well-known words they had heard so often coming from the unoccupied room that the listeners returned to reality. Their faces wore a look of intense expectancy as they listened and heard the message:

> " Hir yw'r dydd,
> A hir yw'r nos."

As they listened, the singer removed his hands from the trembling strings and bowed his head in silence. Then, from another room in the house arose a voice, singing no longer a plaint, but thrilling with accents of triumphant joy :

"A hir yw aros, Arawn."

A long, deep silence followed. It was broken by the grave voice of the stranger, who asked leave to retire. "For," said he, "I am, indeed, weary, and must be up betimes." Then, after wishing the family "nos dawch," he was conducted to his room.

On the following morning the maid, after knocking at the door of the stranger's room, and receiving no answer, reported the fact to her mistress. Fearing some mishap they entered the room. It was empty. The rays of the morning sun, pouring through the open casement, fell on a bed that had not been slept in.

The tall and handsome visitor was never seen again, and never again in the meadows of the Neuadd was the voice heard singing its sad refrain :

"Hir yw'r dydd,
A hir yw'r nos,
A hir yw aros, Arawn."